THE FUN FINANCE FORMULA

THE FUN FINANCE FORMULA

UNLOCK THE SECRET TO GROWING YOUR MONEY AND LOVING EVERY STEP

QUEENIE TAN

WILEY

First published 2025 by John Wiley & Sons Australia, Ltd

© John Wiley & Sons Australia, Ltd 2025

All rights reserved, including rights for text and data mining and training of artificial intelligence technologies or similar technologies. Except as permitted under the *Australian Copyright Act 1968* (for example, a fair dealing for the purposes of study, research, criticism or review) no part of this publication may be reproduced, stored in a retrieval system, or transmitted, in any form or by any means, electronic, mechanical, photocopying, recording or otherwise. Advice on how to obtain permission to reuse material from this title is available at http://www.wiley.com/go/permissions.

The right of Queenie Tan to be identified as the author of *The Fun Finance Formula* has been asserted in accordance with law.

ISBN: 978-1-394-34610-3

A catalogue record for this book is available from the National Library of Australia

Registered Office
John Wiley & Sons Australia, Ltd. Level 4, 600 Bourke Street, Melbourne, VIC 3000, Australia

For details of our global editorial offices, customer services, and more information about Wiley products visit us at www.wiley.com.

Wiley also publishes its books in a variety of electronic formats and by print-on-demand. Some content that appears in standard print versions of this book may not be available in other formats.

Trademarks: Wiley and the Wiley logo are trademarks or registered trademarks of John Wiley & Sons, Inc. and/or its affiliates in the United States and other countries and may not be used without written permission. All other trademarks are the property of their respective owners. John Wiley & Sons, Inc. is not associated with any product or vendor mentioned in this book.

Limit of Liability/Disclaimer of Warranty
While the publisher and author have used their best efforts in preparing this work, they make no representations or warranties with respect to the accuracy or completeness of the contents of this work and specifically disclaim all warranties, including without limitation any implied warranties of merchantability or fitness for a particular purpose. No warranty may be created or extended by sales representatives, written sales materials or promotional statements for this work. This work is sold with the understanding that the publisher is not engaged in rendering professional services. The advice and strategies contained herein may not be suitable for your situation. You should consult with a specialist where appropriate. The fact that an organisation, website, or product is referred to in this work as a citation and/or potential source of further information does not mean that the publisher and author endorse the information or services the organisation, website, or product may provide or recommendations it may make. Further, readers should be aware that websites listed in this work may have changed or disappeared between when this work was written and when it is read. Neither the publisher nor author shall be liable for any loss of profit or any other commercial damages, including but not limited to special, incidental, consequential, or other damages.

Cover and inside cover design by Andy Warren Design

Set in 10.5/14.5pt Utopia Std by Straive, Chennai, India.

SKYE8BC6D64-17FA-4F58-9D75-77FFF788AF02_071525

To my little daughter Gia: May you have the courage to explore and chase your dreams, live life on your own terms and be true to the amazing person who you were always meant to be.

To my partner Pablo: Thank you for being my rock, my biggest ally and my sounding board. Your support (and letting me include some real-life stories about you in here!) means the world to me.

To my parents: Thank you for teaching me two very different but equally important lessons about money. Dad, you showed me the power of saving and investing. Mum, you reminded me that money is meant to be enjoyed.

CONTENTS

About the author	ix
Acknowledgements	xi
Disclaimer	xiii
Introduction	xv
1 **DISCOVER** that money is fun	1
2 Master your money **MINDSET**	19
3 Choose **GRATITUDE** over comparison	39
4 Set **GOALS** that excite you	57
5 Spend with **INTENTION**	75
6 **BALANCE** the 3Fs: Foundation, fun and freedom	97
7 **SAVE** without sucking the fun from life	119
8 **INVEST** with confidence	131
9 Win the **PROPERTY** game	155
10 **TRACK** your wealth for fun	181

11	Take **MINI-RETIREMENTS**	191
12	**PAY IT FORWARD**	207
	Living the Fun Finance Formula	227
	References	231

ABOUT THE AUTHOR

Queenie Tan is a personal finance content creator, entrepreneur and mum dedicated to making money fun and accessible.

Through Invest With Queenie, she helps others break free from financial stress and build wealth effortlessly. When she's not creating content, she enjoys travelling, trying money-saving hacks and spending time with her partner, Pablo, and their daughter, Gia.

Follow Queenie for more money tips: @investwithqueenie on Instagram, TikTok and YouTube.

ACKNOWLEDGEMENTS

I acknowledge the Traditional Custodians of the land on which this book was written, the Eora Nation, and pay my respects to Elders past, present and emerging.

This book would not have been possible without the love, support and encouragement of so many incredible people.

To the team at Wiley: Thank you for believing in this book and helping me bring it to life.

To the Invest With Queenie community: Your support, engagement and questions have shaped so much of this book. I hope it helps you on your journey to financial freedom.

And, finally, to every person who picked up this book: I'm so grateful to be a small part of your financial journey. Here's to making money fun!

DISCLAIMER

The information in this book is general in nature and does not take into account your personal financial circumstances. It is for educational purposes only, and does not constitute personal financial advice or any other professional advice. You should always do your own research and seek professional advice that is tailored to your specific needs and circumstances.

While every effort has been made to ensure the information provided is accurate and up to date at the time of publication, no responsibility is accepted for any loss, injury or inconvenience sustained by any person relying on the information contained in this book.

Queenie Tan is an authorised representative (Number: 1301362) of MoneySherpa Pty Ltd (ABN 32 164 927 708), which holds an Australian Financial Services Licence (AFSL 451289).

The author, publisher, and associated entities disclaim any and all liability for any loss or damage arising directly or indirectly from the use of this book or any errors or omissions in its content.

INTRODUCTION

Growing up, whenever someone at school asked what my dad did for a living, I never quite knew how to answer. My dad didn't have a job — not in the conventional sense anyway. He wasn't rushing off to a 9 to 5 or working late nights in an office. My dad was a single, stay-at-home parent who had retired early. And while most people equate not working with being lazy or struggling, he was far from either of those things. He had achieved what so many people dream of: the freedom to spend his time however he wanted.

As a kid, it didn't feel like we were rich. I went to public schools, we never took holidays, and my dad drove an ancient, loud car that was so embarrassing I'd ask him to drop me off a few streets away from school. We didn't have the flashy stuff other kids had, and I remember wishing we could afford 'nicer' things.

Yet, despite that, I always felt we had *enough*. We had food on the table, bills were paid and I never felt like we were struggling. But behind that sense of stability was a constant tension. You see, my parents had very different approaches to money that were more than just quirky contrasts — they were the main reason they divorced.

After my parents divorced, I lived with my dad and my mum would come visit and stay with us from time to time. It was during these visits that their different philosophies around money became more apparent. My dad, a Malaysian Chinese immigrant, treated saving like a sport. To him, frugality wasn't just a habit — it was a virtue. He'd scour three different shops just to save a few dollars, and every expense was carefully considered. Early retirement was his ultimate prize, and he achieved it through years of meticulous budgeting and self-discipline.

My mum, on the other hand, had a completely different philosophy. As an Australian with Irish-Scottish roots, she believed that money was meant to be enjoyed. She'd spend freely on things that made life fun and comfortable — long phone calls with family, a toasty warm house in winter and little indulgences that brought her joy.

Side note: back in the early 2000s, phone calls were priced per minute. So it wasn't uncommon for those long phone calls to rack up bills of $100 in today's dollars! To Mum, staying connected with loved ones was worth it, but to Dad, the thought of spending so much on a phone bill was unbearable.

While they both approached money in ways that reflected their values, those differing values led to endless arguments. For example, Mum would turn the heating on to make our home cosy during winter, but Dad would insist we wear extra jumpers instead. For Mum, comfort was worth the cost; for Dad, it was an unnecessary expense. These debates may seem small, but they symbolised a deeper divide.

And it's not just my parents — money is one of the leading causes of relationship breakdowns. Studies show that financial disagreements are a major reason for divorce, and it's easy to see why. When two people have vastly different views on spending and saving, it creates tension, resentment and, ultimately, distance.

Growing up, I often felt caught between their opposing worlds. From Dad, I learned the importance of saving, planning and building financial security; from Mum, I learned to appreciate the present and spend money on what truly matters. But, as a child, I didn't understand why money caused so much friction between them, and I didn't understand why they couldn't just find a balance.

It wasn't until I was older that I began to see how their conflict around money shaped me. I became obsessed with finding a balance — something they never quite managed. I didn't want to live so frugally that I missed out on life's joys, but I also didn't want to spend recklessly and jeopardise my future.

More importantly, I didn't want money to dictate my life or my relationships. I wanted the freedom to make choices without having to constantly think about money.

When I got my first job at McDonald's at 14, I thought I was finally on the path to financial independence while earning a solid $10 an hour. Most of that went straight to overpriced smoothies, concert tickets and clothes, but, hey, it felt like freedom. Best of all, I didn't have to ask my dad for money anymore, which felt like asking a brick wall to give you $20. After a few years of working in hospitality and retail, though, I realised one thing: I didn't want to spend my life standing for hours and smiling through awkward customer interactions. My feet were sore, my patience was running thin and I started to wonder ... surely there's a better way?

At first, my paycheques were all about instant gratification — I was living in the moment, just like Mum. But after a while, the thrill of spending started to fade, and I began asking myself, *Where is all my money going?* That's when I stumbled across the concept of investing and passive income. The more I learned, the clearer it became — wealth isn't about hoarding money or pinching every penny, it's about the freedom and flexibility it gives you. It's the ease of knowing you're not chained to a paycheque or stuck in a job just to make ends meet. Real wealth means you get to choose what you do simply because you enjoy it, not because you're worried about how much it costs.

Suddenly, Dad's frugal ways began to make sense. His sacrifices weren't about deprivation, they were about building a life of freedom and not having to rely on a job.

So, you might be wondering — who am I, and why am I writing this book? I'm Queenie, a licensed personal finance content creator (meaning I've earned a licence to give general financial advice). For the past five years, I've been creating educational videos on social media, sharing my journey with money and the lessons I've learned. Over time, I've grown a community of people who want to take control of their finances without sacrificing the things they love. This book is an extension of that journey — a deeper dive into the principles and practices that have helped me build wealth while living a joyful and fulfilling life.

What we've been told about building wealth is wrong. In this book, I'm here to show you that wealth isn't about endless spreadsheets or giving up your daily coffee. It's about making intentional choices, spending on what matters most and enjoying the journey along the way. Whether it's saving for your first home, investing for your future or simply feeling less stressed about money, I'll show you how to master your finances and have fun at the same time.

Because here's the thing: money doesn't have to be stressful. It doesn't have to be a source of guilt or fear. When managed well, money can bring freedom, joy and fun! Just like getting fit means finding an activity you love, building wealth is easiest when you enjoy the process.

This isn't a book about saving and sucking all the happiness from your life. It's about creating a life where money works for you, and I mean literally — you'll learn how to get your money working for you, so you can focus on what truly makes you happy. I'll share stories, strategies and ways to help you get there without sacrificing the things that make life rich right now.

Introduction

The heart of this book is the Fun Finance Formula, a game-changing tool designed to transform the way you think about money. It will help you build lasting financial confidence and set yourself up for a stronger, more secure future.

In each chapter you're going to learn one piece of the Fun Finance Formula, so by the end of the book, you'll be ready to build wealth on your own terms, and enjoy your life at the same time.

So, let's get started. Whether you're just beginning your financial journey or you've been building wealth for years, this book will show you that building wealth and having fun don't have to be opposites. In fact, they go hand in hand.

Chapter 1
DISCOVER that money is fun

I always thought my dad was a bit sad when it came to money, because he didn't enjoy spending money like other people did. His showers aren't really showers. He turned on the water so slightly you'd think there was a plumbing issue. And his toothbrush looked like it had survived an explosion. And don't get me started on the free McDonald's napkins he's been hoarding since I was a child. To me, money was meant to be enjoyed; to him, spending was something to be avoided. And I saw that as a problem until one night at dinner when I had a realisation that completely flipped my perspective — and, honestly, it blew my mind.

I had my dad over for dinner, and we were sitting across from each other, both buzzing with excitement but for completely different reasons. He was describing his latest project: landscaping his front yard. He spoke with the kind of energy most people reserve for their latest adventure, talking about the perfect spot for a lemon tree, how he contacted three different landscapers and managed to find one within his budget.

Meanwhile, I was equally excited, sharing my latest investment plans for my baby daughter. I had recently started building a portfolio for her with the ambitious goal of making her a millionaire. As I talked about investing, compound interest and my strategy for her financial future, it hit me:

We were both having fun.

The way my dad and I talk to each other about money is the way some people talk to their dads about sport.

For my dad, saving money and hunting for deals wasn't just about being frugal, it was his version of a treasure hunt. He found joy in every dollar saved, every clever bargain and every well-thought-out decision. For me, building wealth through investing wasn't a chore, it was exciting.

That moment reframed everything I thought about money. It doesn't have to be sad, stressful or dull; it can be creative, fulfilling and fun. Saving, investing and spending wisely aren't just about the end goal, they're about enjoying the process, finding excitement in the journey and aligning your financial choices with what you value most.

That realisation changed how I view wealth-building. It's not about deprivation — it's about fun. And when you approach money with the right mindset, it becomes not just a means to an end, but a source of joy.

What's coming up next...

In this chapter, we'll:

- redefine your relationship with money, focusing on joy and purpose
- explore the idea of purpose-driven finances, aligning your spending and saving with what truly matters to you

- introduce practical exercises to help you uncover your *why* and create financial goals that excite you
- share real-life examples of how reframing your mindset can transform how you approach wealth-building.

By the end of this chapter, you'll see money as a tool to build the life you want, rather than a source of stress or limitation.

The different types of money

When you ask people to describe money, you can get some very different responses. To some people, money is the root of all evil, and to others, money is good and can be used to help them achieve their dreams.

But here's an idea that will change how you think about money: all these perspectives are correct because there are different types of money. There's happy money and sad money, as money and happiness expert Ken Honda would say, but I believe there's more to it. I like to think of it as fun money and heavy money, but money can also be lucky or skilful. Let me explain.

Fun money vs heavy money

Fun money is the kind you earn or spend with joy. Think of a Christmas gift from your grandma or a paycheque from a job you love. It's money that feels good, uplifting and positive. For example, when I set up an investment account for my daughter on her birthday, I felt so much joy knowing I was doing something meaningful for her future. And when she receives that money, she will feel its happy energy. That's fun money. Whenever you can, aim to give and receive fun money.

On the other hand, my parents spent a lot of money in court when they got divorced, and this was money they both regretted spending. That was *heavy money*—money tied to stress and unhappiness. Like paying for a parking ticket or earning money from a job that drains you, it leaves you stressed, frustrated or regretful. Heavy money weighs you down. It makes building wealth feel like a burden, draining your motivation. This perpetuates the cycle of heavy money.

This is why some people think money is evil, because sometimes it can be. To them, money might only remind them of sad experiences. But as we've seen (and I'm sure you've felt this too), money can also be good. It can bring happiness and be used in ways that feel uplifting, positive and joyful.

The goal is simple: try to create and use as much fun money as possible. Sometimes, heavy money is unavoidable — life happens after all — and sometimes things happen that you can't predict, but when you make an effort to earn, spend and give money in ways that feel good, money becomes something positive — not just for you, but for others too.

This shift makes building wealth easier and guilt-free. When you earn fun money from work you enjoy, it feels fulfilling. When you spend it joyfully, you pass that positive energy to others, creating a cycle of fun money.

So, in short, strive to earn and spend fun money. Not only will it help you build wealth with ease, but it will also spread positivity and joy to those around you, continuing the cycle of happy money.

But here's the thing: not all fun money is in your control. Some money takes effort, while other money feels lucky. That's where the real magic happens — understanding the overlap of these types.

Lucky money vs skilled money

Lucky money feels effortless and happens by chance. You have little control over this money: it might come from winning the lottery, receiving an unexpected gift, making a risky investment on a random meme coin and doubling your money overnight, or inheriting money from a rich Nigerian prince you didn't know you were related to. Lucky money flows naturally, without much effort or planning on your part.

The downside to lucky money is its unpredictability. It's hard to replicate or scale, and since it's tied to external factors, you can't control when it happens or if it happens again.

Skilled money, on the other hand, is money earned through deliberate effort, knowledge or expertise. It's the money you work long hours for, learn new skills for and figure out ways to build creative systems for.

Skilled money takes effort upfront but, once mastered, it can often transform into something more consistent and reliable. Of course, some luck is still involved in order to succeed, but you have much more control over it compared with lucky money. For example, building a business or learning to invest takes time and dedication, but over time, it creates opportunities for consistent returns. Skilled money is more fulfilling because it's tied to your abilities, giving you more confidence in your financial future. And the best part is, it gets easier over time.

Hard choices, easy life; easy choices, hard life

There's a personal development quote from Jerzy Gregorek that I love: 'Hard choices, easy life. Easy choices, hard life.' The way I interpret it is that taking the easy path now often makes life harder in the long run, while making hard choices today sets you up for an easier future.

Let's think about something as mundane as brushing your teeth. If you skip brushing for a day, it's no big deal. Nothing disastrous happens. You're not going to wake up the next morning with your teeth falling out. But what if you didn't brush for a year? Or five years? Things start to change. You might get cavities, your gums might bleed or you may even lose teeth. Suddenly, what seemed like a small, easy choice in the moment has snowballed into painful dentist visits, costly treatments or permanent damage. The 'easy' choice of not brushing becomes the 'hard' reality of dealing with the consequences.

Now let's apply this to money. Spending everything you earn in the present often feels easy. Treating yourself, eating out and buying things you don't really need can feel good in the moment. But if you consistently choose to spend instead of saving or investing, future you ends up with a much harder life. Unexpected expenses, missed opportunities or a lack of financial freedom can weigh you down when it matters most.

On the flip side, making the hard choice to save, budget or invest today takes effort. But those small, disciplined actions add up to big rewards over time. Hard choices such as sticking to a budget, paying off high-interest debt or investing lead to financial freedom, stability and the ability to live life on your terms.

The lesson here isn't about deprivation or living in fear of the future; it's about finding balance. You don't need to give up all the joys of today for tomorrow's security. Instead, ask yourself: *How can I balance enjoying life now while still setting myself up for the future I want?*

This principle applies to both money and life in general. The choices you make today shape the life you'll have tomorrow. The key is to be intentional, even when it's hard, because those hard choices are what make the easy life possible.

The four money types

Imagine drawing a line down the middle of a piece of paper. At the top, you write *fun money*, and at the bottom, *heavy money*. Then, draw another line across the middle. To the left, write *lucky money*, and to the right, *skilled money*.

Now you've got four quadrants:

- Fun and lucky money
- Fun and skilled money

- Heavy and lucky money
- Heavy and skilled money

Let's have a look at each one (see figure 1.1).

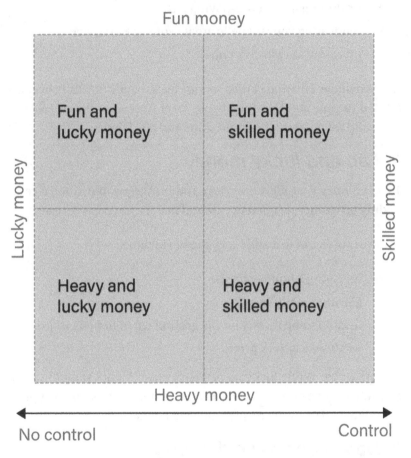

Figure 1.1: The four money quadrants

1. Fun and skilled money

This is the most rewarding quadrant. It's money you've earned through effort, expertise or systems, and it aligns with your values and goals. This is exactly what author Simon Sinek means when he says, 'Working hard for something you hate is called stress, and working hard for something you love is called passion.'

Some examples of fun and skilled money include:

- working hard to save for your dream home
- starting a passion-driven business
- upskilling for a better-paying job
- renovating your home to create your dream space
- investing in your retirement.

Key takeaway: Fun and skilled money feels deeply fulfilling because it's tied to your abilities and efforts. Over time, it becomes easier to scale and replicate as you build skills and confidence.

2. Fun and lucky money

This is money that feels effortless and brings joy, but since it relies mainly on chance, it's tied to external factors you can't control.

Some examples of fun and lucky money include:

- receiving a holiday bonus
- getting a birthday gift
- finding some money on the ground when nobody is around
- winning a lottery prize.

Key takeaway: While lucky money feels great, it's not something you can rely on consistently. Treat it as a bonus and use it to support your financial goals or create joyful experiences.

3. Heavy and skilled money

This quadrant is tough. It's money you've worked hard to earn or manage, but it's tied to stress, unhappiness or misalignment with your values. Don't worry, I've been there.

You'll know you're earning heavy and skilled money when you're:

- working long hours at a job you dislike
- taking on a second job you hate to cover bills

- paying off high-interest debt
- covering unexpected medical bills
- making overdue car or home repairs.

Key takeaway: Heavy and skilled money might feel draining in the short term, but it can often serve as a stepping stone to happy money. If you can redirect this money toward meaningful goals, you'll gradually shift to the fun money quadrants.

4. Heavy and lucky money

This is the most frustrating quadrant. It's money that comes to you unexpectedly but carries regret, guilt or emotional baggage.

Heavy and lucky money may fall into the following categories:

- receiving an inheritance after losing a loved one
- getting a severance package after being made redundant at work
- getting scammed because you thought you were in a relationship with Brad Pitt
- paying fines or fees for missed deadlines.

Key takeaway: Heavy and lucky money often feels fleeting and unsatisfying. To avoid this quadrant, focus on creating skills-based money systems that bring more stability and control.

Figure 1.2 (overleaf) shows how these quadrants map together.

The dream quadrant is the fun and skilled money quadrant. Because while lucky and fun money feels great, it's outside of your control since it relies on chance.

Let's look at an example: The odds of winning the Powerball jackpot in Australia are one in 134 490 400, which means if you buy a lotto ticket, you have a 99.99999926 per cent chance of losing money. To put this into perspective, you are approximately 134 times more likely to be struck by lightning than to win the Powerball jackpot in Australia.

THE FUN FINANCE FORMULA

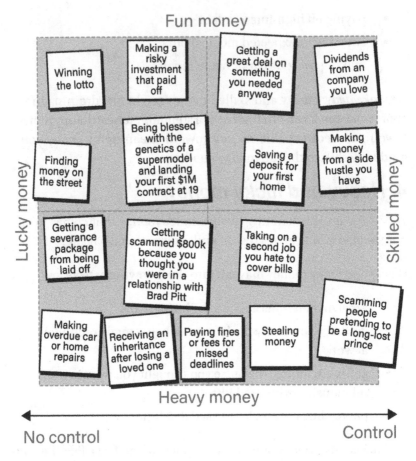

Figure 1.2: Example of mapping the four quadrants

Now let's compare that to the odds on making money from a smart investment, which is in the top right-hand corner (fun and skilled money). Global investment manager Capital Group analysed 94 years worth of data and concluded that the odds of making a positive return on an S&P 500 exchange traded funds (ETFs, which is the top 500 companies in the US) drastically increase the longer you remain invested. Over one year you have a 73 per cent chance of a positive return. But if you hold it for five years, that number jumps up to 88 per cent. But what about if you hold it for ten years? The number jumps up to 94 per cent!

So by focusing on the fun and skilled quadrant, we can stack the odds in our favour by focusing on what we can control. And when we develop our skills and become more skilled, we can more easily replicate and scale this kind of fun money.

The Fun Finance Formula will help you to focus on stacking the odds in your favour by focusing on the money you can control in the fun money quadrant.

Why we shouldn't chase the fun and lucky money

Let me take you back to my childhood when I was a full-time comparison expert and part-time envy enthusiast. One of my friends had what I thought was *the life*. Her house was immaculate. Every room smelled like vanilla or something fancy, thanks to those expensive candles you only see in magazines. The furniture actually matched — like it came straight out of a catalogue. And her parents? Always cheerful, always laughing, like they were in a TV show. I mean, who laughs that much while doing dishes?

Then, there was my house. We had weeds growing taller than me out the front. Our furniture was basically a mismatched ensemble of street-side finds. My dad called it 'eclectic', but I'm pretty sure the correct name for it was 'disjointed'. And while we technically had a pool in the backyard, it was more of a science experiment. My dad decided maintaining it was too much effort, so he drained it. Nature took over, and it became this swampy green rainwater pit complete with a dead frog.

And don't get me started on Christmas. While my friend was decked out in matching family pyjamas taking pictures in their beautiful house, my dad and I didn't really do the whole festive thing. As an only child living with a single parent, it was pretty lonely. The highlight of our holiday season was probably eating a slightly fancier dinner in front of the TV while watching the cricket.

I used to sit there, stewing in my envy, wondering why my life wasn't more like my friend's. Why didn't my house smell like vanilla candles? Why couldn't my dad invest in furniture that matched? And why was there a dead frog in the pool?

But here's the thing: as we got older, I found out my friend's life wasn't as perfect as it seemed. Sure, her house looked great, but behind those matching cushions were some big family struggles. Her parents weren't always as cheerful as they appeared, and sometimes they struggled to make ends meet financially. Their beautiful living room hid a lot of things that weren't quite as dreamy.

And while I didn't feel rich, looking back now, I realise we were rich in ways I didn't appreciate at the time. Sure, our home didn't look like it belonged in a magazine, but my dad didn't need to work. And even though we didn't have many material possessions, I was lucky because I knew all our essentials and needs were covered.

After I moved out, I saved up and bought the Christmas tree of my dreams for my own home — the twinkly kind you see in movies — and decorated it to my heart's content. My efforts actually inspired my dad to finally get rid of the jungle of weeds out front and the swampy pool in the backyard. He even hired a landscaper to redesign the front yard, making it beautiful and much easier to maintain.

So, while my childhood home wasn't magazine-cover ready, it was a symbol of growth, love and transformation.

This is why we shouldn't focus too much on the fun and lucky money. We often hear stories about people who became an overnight success. Maybe they won the lottery or made some risky but lucky investment or they inherited a lot of money, and then we compare ourselves and how we don't measure up. Comparing ourselves to people who seem to have luck on their side only sets us up for frustration, especially since we never see the full picture. We focus on their blessings but ignore their burdens.

Here's the thing...

Chasing lucky money, even the happy kind, is like putting all your hopes on winning the lottery (which, as we established, has a 99.99999926 per cent chance of disappointment). Instead, we should focus on what we can control: building money skills that feel happy and meaningful and that grow over time. It's about stacking the odds in our favour, not crossing our fingers and hoping for the best.

Because, let's face it, dead frogs in a swampy pool might not scream 'luxury', but learning to laugh about it (and focusing on what you can change) sets you up for a much better future.

Finding your financial why: Amanda's story

A few years ago, we hosted one of our very first budgeting workshops. It was an experiment, a chance to share what we'd learned about budgeting and to test out the early product for a budgeting tool we were working on. Around the table were a handful of women, each with unique goals and challenges, but all wanting to take control of their finances.

We started the session by going around the circle, asking everyone to share their financial 'why' — the goal that motivated them to want to improve their money habits. When it was Amanda's turn, she hesitated for a moment before admitting that her dream was to buy her first home. At 27, she was working as an account manager in Sydney, one of the most unaffordable housing markets in the world. On top of that, she still had student debt to pay off, and the constant media chatter about how young people had no chance of buying their own home had left her doubting whether it was even possible.

'I guess it's just a nice thought,' she said, 'but I don't think it's realistic for me right now.'

By the end of the workshop, Amanda had a shift in mindset. She decided to focus not on the things she couldn't control (like the property prices) but on what she could control (such as how she managed her money). She left with a simple plan: start tracking her spending, figure out where her money was really going and see if she could make changes to move closer to her goal.

Over the next few months, Amanda stuck to her plan. She started using our budgeting tool Billroo to track her spending and identify patterns. That's when she realised how much money was slipping away on things she didn't truly value, such as clothes and takeaway meals. By cutting back on those areas, she redirected those funds toward her student debt. To her surprise, it only took a few months to pay off her debt completely — a milestone she once thought would take years. The sense of accomplishment was exhilarating.

But then she faced the question: what next? With her student debt gone, Amanda set her sights on her bigger goal: saving for a house deposit. She knew it would take more than just cutting back on spending so she focused on increasing her income. Amanda negotiated a pay rise at work and took on some side hustles. Every extra dollar she earned went straight into her deposit fund.

By tracking her spending and aligning it with her goals, Amanda transformed her relationship with money. The money she used to spend on things she barely noticed (heavy money) was now fun money, fuelling her dreams. Each deposit she made toward her savings account brought her closer to the life she wanted, and the discipline she'd developed along the way made it easier to stay on track.

Within a year, Amanda achieved what she once thought was impossible: she saved enough for her first home deposit and exchanged contracts on her dream property. The key was focusing on the things she could control, making intentional choices and staying committed to her financial 'why'.

Key takeaways from Amanda's story

Identify your 'why': Find a financial goal that excites and motivates you.

- Focus on what you can control: Let go of the things outside your power and channel your energy into what you can change.
- Celebrate small wins: Each step you take, no matter how small, adds up to something bigger over time.

Amanda's journey is proof that with a clear goal, the right mindset and consistent effort, even the biggest financial dreams are within reach.

Your turn: Map your money quadrants

To help you put these ideas into practice, let's map out your current relationship with money. Grab a piece of paper and let's get started.

Divide your page into four quadrants.

- Top left: fun and lucky money
- Top right: fun and skilled money
- Bottom left: heavy and lucky money
- Bottom right: heavy and skilled money

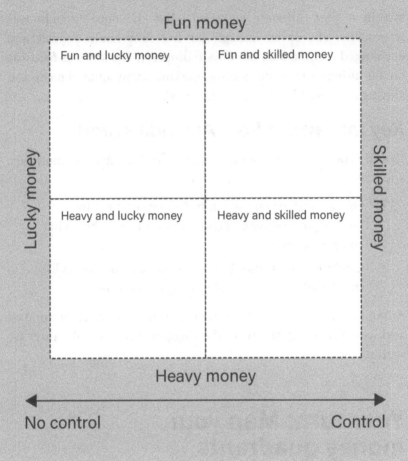

Reflect on your recent money experiences

Think of all the sources of money coming to you this month (money in) and how you've spent it (money out). For each type of money write down two to three examples in the corresponding quadrant. For example:

- Fun and skilled: Paying for a trip you've always wanted to take (money out) or earning a raise at work (money in)
- Fun and lucky: Receiving a surprise bonus or gift or finding a $50 note on the ground (money in) and spending it on a spontaneous round of cocktails for your friends (money out)

- Heavy and skilled: Paying off a stressful debt (money out) or working overtime in a job you dislike (money in)
- Heavy and lucky: Receiving an inheritance from a loss (money in) or paying fines for mistakes (money out)

Analyse your quadrants

- Which quadrant has the most examples?
- Which quadrant do you wish to focus on more?
- Are there areas where you could shift heavy money into fun money or lucky money into skilled money?

Set a money goal

Based on your reflections, set a small, actionable goal to increase your fun and skilled money.

For example: if you've identified spending money on things you don't value (heavy money), decide to redirect that toward saving for a meaningful goal (fun money).

Or, if you've been relying on lucky money, focus on developing a skill to create more skilled money.

Key takeaways

- Money can be fun, creative and fulfilling. Saving and investing can bring as much joy as spending when aligned with your values.
- Wealth isn't about deprivation, it's about creating freedom and choices. True wealth is about using money intentionally to build the life you love.
- Money can be joyful when earned, spent and invested with purpose.
- There's a difference between fun money (uplifting) and heavy money (stressful).
- Relying on lucky money isn't sustainable, so it's important to focus on building skilled money.

In a nutshell

This chapter was all about rethinking your relationship with money and understanding its different types. We explored fun money (money earned or spent with joy) and heavy money (money tied to stress or regret) and introduced the concepts of lucky money (unpredictable and outside your control) and skilled money (earned through effort, knowledge and deliberate action). The key takeaway is that focusing on what you can control and aligning your money with your values leads to more meaningful and fulfilling financial outcomes.

We also mapped out the four money quadrants (fun and skilled, fun and lucky, heavy and skilled, and heavy and lucky) to help you visualise where your money is coming from and going. By prioritising fun and skilled money, you can stack the odds in your favour, develop long-term financial security and unlock the joy of intentional wealth-building.

This chapter also gave you the first piece of the Fun Finance Formula: figuring out that *money can be joyful and fun*. Now that you've unlocked this foundational concept, we'll look at the next step: shifting your money mindset to set yourself up for financial success.

Now you're ready to move on to the next chapter, where we'll explore how your money mindset shapes your financial journey and how to master it to achieve the life you want.

Chapter 2
Master your money MINDSET

Look around you. Everything in your life right now was once just a thought in your mind. That's the power of your mindset. The way you think about money can either propel you toward the life you've always dreamed of or quietly hold you back. And here's the crazy thing—you might not even realise it's happening. This came into focus when my partner, Pablo, and I decided to upgrade our home.

Our daughter had just joined our family, and we needed a bigger space to grow into. This wasn't the first time we'd been house hunting. Five years earlier, we were in a completely different financial situation, looking at the cheapest apartments we could find in Sydney. These were one- or two-bedroom places—many of them old, needing major renovations or riddled with issues—because that's all we could afford at the time.

I still remember some of those inspections like it was yesterday. At this one place, the tenants were still asleep in the bedrooms. The real estate agent, bless them, was acting like it was totally normal. So, one by one, all the potential buyers shuffled up to the slightly cracked door and awkwardly peeked in. At another, we left the building and I had that eerie feeling of being watched. I turned around and, sure enough, there was a creepy-looking man peering at me through the slits in his blinds in the dark. It was like something out of a horror movie!

Fast forward to this new chapter in our lives, and things had changed significantly. Thanks to the power of investing, compound interest and a bit of luck, Pablo and I were in a completely different financial position. This time, the homes we were inspecting were light years ahead — spacious, modern and perfectly suited for our growing family. And, let me tell you, there were no sleeping tenants or creepy men watching us from behind blinds in these places (at least none that I could see)!

But as we walked through these beautiful homes, I noticed something surprising: instead of feeling excited, I felt…uncomfortable. I remember walking into one particular home. It was stunning — light-filled, modern and exactly what we needed — and, as I stepped into the living room, my first thought wasn't about how perfect it was for us. Instead, I thought, *Wow, this place is really nice, but it's too nice for us.*

Hearing those words in my head stopped me in my tracks. Why did I think that? Why was I telling myself that this home — a home we could afford and had worked hard for — was somehow 'too good' for us? It didn't make sense.

The more I reflected on it, the clearer it became that this was a limiting belief. Pablo and I had been conditioned by our upbringings to think this way. We were both only children raised in single-parent households. My dad, as you might remember from Chapter 1, was incredibly frugal and financially savvy. Pablo's mum, who raised him on her own, had a similar approach to money. Both of us grew up with a mindset of spending the bare minimum, saving as much as possible and always choosing the cheapest option.

Even during the early years of our relationship, we carried this mindset with us. When we were saving for our first home, we wouldn't order anything at cafes or restaurants if we were out with friends, just to save money. That habit of scrimping and saving had shaped how we saw ourselves: as people who couldn't afford nice things, who didn't deserve to spend money on ourselves.

And so, when we walked into that beautiful home, a part of me still believed that narrative. Even though we had grown our wealth, I still thought, *This is too nice for us.*

But here's the thing: that belief wasn't true. And, fortunately, I caught myself in the moment. I reminded myself that the reason we were inspecting homes like this was because we could afford it. This wasn't about showing off—it was about recognising that we had outgrown our old financial limits and deserved to enjoy our next chapter in life.

I'm happy to say that we ended up buying that home. Today, we're so grateful we challenged that belief because it allowed us to step into the life we'd been working toward all along.

Why limiting beliefs matter

That experience taught me something powerful: the way we think about money can quietly shape our decisions and hold us back from enjoying the life we've earned. Without even realising it, these deep-seated beliefs limit us and keep us stuck in a cycle of doubt and scarcity, even when you've already outgrown it.

Limiting beliefs are many and varied, but they often appear in the themes of self-worth, scarcity, work, money, risk and success. Here are some examples.

I'm bad with money

Impact: Leads to self-doubt, causing you to avoid managing finances and miss out on growth opportunities.

Replacement thought: I'm learning to manage my money better.

I don't deserve nice things

Impact: Makes you undervalue your achievements, settling for less and feeling guilty when you spend money on yourself.

Replacement thought: I am worthy of abundance and I deserve to enjoy the money I've worked hard for, and things that bring me happiness and comfort.

Money is hard to make

Impact: Traps you in a scarcity mindset, leading to overwork, fear of financial risks and constant money stress.

Replacement thought: There are endless ways to make money that align with my skills and my passions. I just need to figure out which direction I want to take and give it a go.

• • •

In this chapter, we're going to explore how these beliefs — like the one I had — can sabotage your financial success. We'll look at four main categories of money filters identified in a fascinating study, and I'll help you uncover which ones might be influencing your decisions. Once you've identified them, we'll work on reframing those beliefs so they serve you, rather than hold you back.

Because here's the truth: money isn't neutral. It comes with baggage and some of it's good and some of it's bad. In working on your money mindset, you will become self-aware and identify those beliefs that are limiting your potential.

What's coming up next...

This chapter examines the idea that your mindset is the foundation of your financial success. Together, we'll explore:

- how limiting beliefs about money can hold you back
- ways to reframe money as a neutral tool that reflects your intentions
- the role of the 'shadow self' and how it reveals your true desires
- why self-sabotage happens and how to overcome it
- how to cultivate a mindset of abundance and joy.

Rewrite your money story

What do you think about money? Maybe you believe money is the root of all evil, or perhaps you think more money will make you happy. Or maybe you tie your self-worth to it, believing your value equals your net worth.

Now, what if I told you that these beliefs could shape every financial decision you make — how you save, spend and even think about wealth? And here's the crazy thing: your beliefs about money might not even be true.

This brings us to a fascinating study that uncovered how our subconscious beliefs about money (money filters) affect our financial health in ways we might not even realise.

Understanding your money filters

Imagine taking a test that reveals your hidden relationship with money. This is exactly what Dr Brad Klontz and his team set out to create in their groundbreaking study. They wanted to understand why some people struggle with money, even when they're financially stable, while others seem to thrive regardless of their circumstances.

In their research, Klontz and his team categorised these into four main scripts (which I like to call 'money filters'). But instead of just listing them, we'll explore how they show up in real life.

1. The 'money is bad' filter

Beliefs: Money is the root of all evil or I don't deserve to be wealthy.

How this shows up: People with this mindset may feel guilty about earning or spending money, struggle with financial planning or self-sabotage their financial growth.

Real-life examples

- *Avoiding promotions:* Turning down a higher-paying job because they feel guilty about making 'too much'.
- *Refusing to invest*: Believing that wealth is corrupting, they avoid learning about investing, thinking it's 'greedy' or 'morally wrong'.
- *Undercharging for services:* Freelancers or business owners may drastically under-price their work because they don't believe they 'deserve' more money.
- *Guilt around spending:* Even when they have savings, they feel anxious about treating themselves, thinking it's 'wasteful' or 'selfish'.

How to break free

Shift the mindset to 'Money is a tool and it can be used in generous ways that can amplify good things in the world'. If you're a kind person, having more money can allow you to help more people. And you can earn and spend money in ways that align with your values and perpetuate this cycle of good money.

2. The 'more money will make me more happy' filter

Belief: If I just had more money, I'd have no problems.

How this shows up: This filter often leads to overworking, overspending and burnout, with the belief that hitting a certain money milestone will finally bring happiness.

Real-life examples

- *Workaholic tendencies:* Constantly chasing the next promotion or business deal even at the cost of health and relationships.
- *Impulse spending for a dopamine hit:* Buying expensive things (luxury cars, designer bags, high-end gadgets) for a temporary happiness boost.
- *'I'll be happy when…' mentality:* Tying happiness to a future financial milestone (e.g., 'I'll be happy when…' or 'I'll enjoy life once I retire').
- *Neglecting non-financial joys:* Prioritising work and money over hobbies, friendships and self-care.

How to break free

Ask yourself: 'Would I still be happy if I had this money, but couldn't spend time with the people I love?' Research shows that experiences and relationships, more so than money, bring lasting happiness (more on this in Chapter 5).

3. The 'money is my self-worth' filter

Belief: My value as a person is based on how much I earn or my net worth.

How it shows up: People with this filter tie their identity and self-esteem to their financial status.

Real-life examples

- *Unhealthy competition:* Feeling pressure to upgrade homes, cars and lifestyles to keep up with friends or peers.
- *Fear of financial failure:* Feeling deep shame if they lose money, experience job loss or have financial struggles.
- *Spending to impress:* Buying luxury items or picking up the bill for others to showcase status.
- *Avoiding financial help:* Refusing to ask for support or talk about money struggles because they see it as a personal failure.

How to break free

Redefine success! True wealth is much more than just money. It's more about the things that money can't buy that bring lasting happiness, fulfilment and security. Like your health and well-being, genuine relationships, a sense of purpose, memories and experiences, personal growth and happiness.

4. The 'extreme frugality' filter

Belief: Saving money is my top priority above all else.

How it shows up: While being mindful of spending is great, extreme frugality can lead to anxiety, hoarding money, and missing out on life's joys.

Real-life examples

- *Never enjoying the money you've worked hard for:* Having large savings but feeling too scared to spend on anything fun.
- *Feeling anxiety around spending:* Overthinking every purchase, even small ones, and feeling guilty for buying non-essentials.
- *Delaying joy indefinitely:* 'I'll travel when I retire' or 'I'll treat myself once I hit $1 million', but never actually doing it.
- *Refusing to invest out of fear:* Keeping all money in cash instead of growing it through investments because of the fear of losing it.

How to break free

Balance is key! Remember that you only have one life, and it's okay to spend on things that bring you joy. Perhaps you could build out a spending plan to ensure it doesn't derail your finances and so you can spend guilt-free on fun, intentional purchases that align with your values.

Which one are you?

Now as we have gone through each of the filters, you're probably nodding your head in agreement and leaning more towards one or two of these money filters.

I can honestly say I've resonated with all of these money filters at some point in my life! But the two that stand out the most for me right now are the extreme frugality filter and the 'more money will make me happy' filter. I love saving, watching my wealth grow, and feeling financially secure — but at the same time, I can get caught up in the idea that reaching the next financial milestone will make me happy, when in reality it actually leads me to a cycle of never being content and never enjoying the milestones I have hit!

Your beliefs about money shape your financial reality — but having a mild inclination toward these filters isn't necessarily a bad thing! For example, a little frugality can help you build wealth, and ambition can push you to achieve great things. The issue arises when these beliefs become extreme and start controlling your decisions, holding you back from financial freedom or happiness.

The good news is, once we become aware of these filters, we can take control instead of letting them dictate our lives. The first step is figuring out which money filter is shaping your decisions. Once you uncover your money beliefs, you can challenge and reframe them to build a mindset that truly works for you. Take the quiz overleaf to discover your money filter.

Your turn: Test your money filter

Are you curious about your own money filter? Here are a few questions inspired by the Klontz money script inventory. Choose the response which aligns most with your point of view. And remember — there are no wrong answers!

1. When you think about your financial future, your first thought is...
   a) I hope I don't make bad money decisions.
   b) I just need to make more money, and everything will fall into place.
   c) I want to be seen as financially successful.
   d) I need to make sure I have enough savings to feel secure.

2. If I suddenly received $100 000, my first instinct would be to...
   a) give some away because I feel uneasy about having it.
   b) treat myself because I finally have the means to enjoy life.
   c) invest or use it in a way that improves my financial reputation.
   d) save it immediately — who knows what could happen?

3. I believe money is...
   a) stressful and often a source of problems.
   b) the key to happiness and a better life.
   c) a measure of success and accomplishment.
   d) something to be carefully protected and managed.

4. When I see someone driving an expensive car, I think:
   a) That's excessive. Do they really need that?
   b) I'd love that — having more money would make life easier.

    c) They must be successful. I wonder what they do for work.

    d) I hope they have a solid emergency fund.

5. When I think about spending money on myself, I feel...

    a) guilty, like I should be doing something more responsible with it.

    b) excited! Money is meant to be enjoyed.

    c) proud — especially if I'm buying something high quality.

    d) a little uneasy, unless it's something really necessary.

6. My biggest fear when it comes to money is...

    a) becoming greedy or selfish if I have too much of it.

    b) never making enough to live the life I truly want.

    c) not earning enough to be respected or successful.

    d) losing what I've worked so hard to save.

7. I believe wealthy people are generally...

    a) out of touch with the struggles of everyday life.

    b) living their best lives — I wish I could do the same.

    c) smart and capable — they must have done something right.

    d) cautious and strategic — that's how they stay rich.

8. If a friend asked me to invest in their new business idea, I'd...

    a) worry about them losing money — it's too risky.

    b) be tempted — if it takes off, I could make a fortune.

    c) consider it, but only if it enhances my financial reputation.

    d) say no — my savings are for security, not speculation.

9. When I see a sale, my first thought is:

    a) I probably don't need anything.

    b) Great! Now's my chance to get what I want.

    c) Time to grab high-quality items at a good price.

    d) Sales are dangerous — I don't want to waste money.

10. If I lost my job tomorrow, I would...
   a) feel like I'd never financially recover.
   b) panic — I'd have no idea how to keep up my lifestyle.
   c) worry about what others would think of me.
   d) be stressed, but at least I'd have my savings to fall back on.

Results

- *Mostly As: The money is bad filter*

  You may associate money with stress or even guilt, believing that wealth can lead to greed or corruption. You likely avoid thinking about finances too much, but deep down, money plays a bigger role in your emotions than you might realise.

- *Mostly Bs: The more money will make me happy filter*

  You may believe that money is the key to happiness and that having more of it would solve most of your problems. While money can improve life, true financial freedom also comes from how you manage it — not just how much you have.

- *Mostly Cs: The money is my self-worth filter*

  You connect wealth with success and self-worth. To you, money isn't just about security — it's about achievement. While financial success can be fulfilling, real confidence comes from within, not just your net worth.

- *Mostly Ds: The extreme frugality filter*

  You see money as something to protect and manage carefully. You're a saver at heart and might even feel uneasy about spending. While financial caution is smart, it's important to enjoy life, too!

Why it matters

Mastering your money script is the second step in the Fun Finance Formula. When you understand the beliefs that drive your decisions, you can start to question them. Are they helping you or holding you back? Our beliefs about money aren't facts — they're stories, and like any story, they can be rewritten.

Your shadow self and what it teaches you

Let's talk about something we all have but rarely think about: our shadow self. This idea comes from the Swiss psychologist Carl Jung, who believed that we all have a side of ourselves that we hide — even from ourselves. The shadow self holds the traits, thoughts or desires we've been taught aren't okay to show to the world. It might include difficult emotions like anger, envy or greed, but it can also include hidden strengths or dreams that we've pushed aside.

The shadow self develops when we're young. As kids, we learn what's 'good' or 'bad' from our families, teachers and society. If you were told that certain feelings — like anger — weren't acceptable, you might have pushed those feelings down. But the shadow self doesn't just disappear, it stays with you, influencing how you think, feel and act in ways you might not even realise.

The shadow self shows up most clearly in how we judge others. Traits we dislike — or envy — in other people often reflect something unresolved within ourselves. Let me share two examples, one from Pablo and one from me, to bring this to life.

Pablo's example: The Instagram flex

Picture this: you're scrolling through Instagram, and you see *that guy*. You know the one. He's got a Rolex on his wrist, casually resting on the steering wheel of some ridiculously expensive car. The caption is something like, 'Another deal closed'.

It's not even subtle. He's clearly trying to flex, but he's acting like he's not. Pablo sees a post like that, rolls his eyes, and immediately thinks, *Wow, what a show-off. Why does he need to flex on everyone like that?* But here's the thing: deep down, what might this be telling Pablo? Maybe, just maybe, he wishes he had the kind of confidence to show off his wins — or even buy a car like that in the first place. His shadow self, the part of him that says, 'Don't draw too much attention to yourself', might actually be craving the spotlight.

Queenie's example: The last slice of pizza

Now, let's talk about me and put it all on the table. Imagine you're out at dinner with friends, and there's one slice of pizza left. Not just any slice, either—the *good one*. The one from your favourite kind of pizza. A big slice too, with a lot of melted cheese. You've been eyeing it for a while, mentally debating whether to grab it. But you don't. You sit there, convincing yourself that you're being polite, that someone else probably wants it more than you.

Five minutes later, you think, maybe it's time. Clearly, nobody wants it. But then your friend swoops in and takes it—just like that. No hesitation, no 'Does anyone want this?' Just pure, unapologetic confidence. As they happily munch away, looking at you, like nothing happened, you're sitting there, silently judging: *Wow, so bold. Who does that?* But, if I'm being honest with myself, my shadow self was showing up big time. Deep down, I wish I had the guts to just go for it without worrying about what anyone else might think. Instead, I let the fear of being *that person* hold me back.

We've all been there, quietly judging someone else when, in reality, our shadow self is just holding up a mirror. The things we envy or dislike in others often reveal what we're suppressing or wishing for in ourselves. And the moment you recognise that, it's a total game-changer.

Recognising your shadow self isn't about blaming yourself—it's about understanding yourself better. When you see those judgements as mirrors of your own thoughts or feelings, you can start to uncover what's really going on beneath the surface.

A story of the shadow self in action

This happened to my aunty, and it's the perfect example of how the shadow self can affect your finances and your life. For years, she worked as a nurse. It was a reliable job but it left her feeling stressed and unfulfilled. Deep down, she disliked wealthy people, often saying things like, 'Rich people don't understand real life', or 'They're so out of touch'.

But one day, her perspective shifted, and it changed her life. While working in a hospital, she spent time with a group of surgeons — professionals earning significantly more than her, with some making upwards of $400 000 a year. She was surprised to find that they weren't selfish or arrogant like she'd imagined. They were kind, approachable and genuinely excited about their lives. They spoke about their families and future plans with joy, exuding energy and purpose.

Meanwhile, many of her colleagues were burned out and stuck in cycles of frustration — feelings she knew all too well. For the first time, my aunty realised her judgement of wealthy people wasn't about them — it was about her. Deep down, her shadow self envied their freedom and ease. Her frustration wasn't really directed at them; it was rooted in her own suppressed desires for a better life.

This realisation changed everything. She started to challenge her own beliefs and became open to new possibilities. Soon after, she was offered a consulting role in the medical industry that allowed her to double her salary and leave behind the job that had been draining her. By acknowledging her shadow self, she was able to rewrite her narrative and take control of her life.

The role of self-sabotage

The shadow self doesn't just reveal your hidden desires — it can also drive self-sabotage. This happens when your old beliefs clash with your goals. For example, if you grew up in a household where money was tight, achieving financial success might feel unfamiliar or uncomfortable. Without even realising it, you might overspend, avoid financial planning or hesitate to take opportunities that could help you move forward.

If you think back to earlier in this chapter when Pablo and I were house hunting, and we toured that beautiful home where my first thought was, *This place is too nice for us*. That belief almost held us back from buying a home that was perfect for our family.

This is classic self-sabotage. My shadow self, shaped by years of frugality and scarcity thinking, was trying to pull me back to the familiar — a place where spending on 'nice' things felt wrong. But by becoming aware of that pattern, I was able to challenge it and make a decision that aligned with the life we'd worked so hard to create.

How to use your shadow self

The shadow self isn't something to fear — it's a powerful tool for self-awareness. It can show you what you value, what you're afraid of and where you need to grow. Here's how you can start working with it:

- *Notice your judgements:* The next time you catch yourself judging someone, pause and ask, *What does this say about me?* Your shadow might be pointing out a hidden desire or fear.
- *Pay attention to admiration:* The traits you admire in others often mirror your own potential. If you're inspired by someone's generosity or confidence, it might mean you have those traits within you, waiting to be nurtured.
- *Reflect on your patterns:* Think about moments when you've sabotaged your own progress. Were you holding yourself back because of an old belief or fear? What might your shadow self be trying to tell you?

Carl Jung believed that integrating the shadow self (acknowledging and accepting the parts of yourself you've buried) is the key to personal growth and wholeness. When you shine a light on your shadow, you can uncover the beliefs and patterns that might be holding you back and transform them into strengths, and create a life that aligns with your true potential.

Your turn: Rewrite your money story

Here's how to start building a winning money mindset.

Document your beliefs

Write down everything you believe about money, both positive and negative. Look for patterns: are they positive, negative or neutral?

Reframe your thoughts

Turn negative statements into empowering ones. For example, instead of saying:

- 'Money is stressful', say 'Money gives me options'.
- 'I'm bad with money', say 'I'm learning to manage money effectively'.

Challenge your shadow self

Reflect on what triggers you about others. Are you jealous of someone's success? Do you harbour fears around not having enough? Use that as a clue to uncover your own desires and set actionable goals.

Break the cycle of self-sabotage

Identify behaviours that hold you back, whether it's overspending, procrastination or perfectionism. Replace these habits with small, consistent actions that align with your goals. For example:

- If you're overspending: Try distancing yourself from your purchases and give yourself a 24-hour limit before you buy non-essential items. That way you can give yourself time to decide if you really want it or not.
- If you're procrastinating your finances: Set up a regular money check-in once per week or month to check in on your finances, even if it's just for ten minutes!

If you're feeling guilty about spending on yourself: Create a 'fun money' budget so you can spend guilt-free on things that make you happy.

Adopt an abundance mindset

Shift your focus from scarcity to abundance (more on this in Chapter 12). Practise gratitude by saying 'thank you' whenever you receive or spend money. This simple habit reinforces a positive relationship with your finances.

Your new money mindset

Your beliefs about money shape your financial reality. By recognising and rewriting these beliefs, you can stop sabotaging yourself and start creating a life that aligns with your goals and values.

Key takeaways

- Your money mindset shapes your reality: The way you think about money influences your financial decisions and the life you create.
- Limiting beliefs hold you back: Beliefs such as 'I don't deserve this' or 'Money is bad' can sabotage your progress, but they're just stories, not facts, and can be rewritten.
- Money scripts drive your habits: The four money filters (see page 24) shape how you view and manage money. Understanding yours is the first step to change.
- The shadow self reflects hidden desires: The traits you envy or dislike in others often reveal what you secretly want for yourself. Recognising this is key to growth.
- Self-sabotage stems from old beliefs: Fear or discomfort from outdated beliefs can hold you back. Awareness helps you break the cycle.
- Money is a tool you can use to fuel your goals and values.

In a nutshell

This chapter was all about mastering your money mindset and uncovering the hidden beliefs that shape your financial decisions. We explored how limiting beliefs (like feeling undeserving of wealth or believing money is inherently bad) can hold you back, and how to reframe these thoughts to align with your goals.

We also introduced the concept of money filters (money is bad, more money will make me happy, money equals self-worth, and extreme frugality) and how they subconsciously influence your financial habits. By identifying which filter affects you the most, you can start reshaping your relationship with money and avoid self-sabotage.

This chapter also introduced the idea of the shadow self — how the qualities we judge or envy in others often reflect our own hidden desires. By understanding and integrating your shadow self, you can break free from negative money patterns and step into financial confidence.

Now that you've uncovered how your beliefs influence your financial reality, the next step is learning how to choose gratitude over comparison. In the next chapter, we're flipping the script on comparison — instead of letting comparison drain your happiness, we'll show you how to use it as a powerful tool for self-reflection.

Chapter 3
Choose **GRATITUDE** over comparison

When I was a kid, the way I measured wealth was pretty simple: Foxtel. And for those who don't know, Foxtel was a pay TV subscription that existed before Netflix. It still exists, but way more people used it back in the early 2000s. The family that had all the channels to me were *rich*, rich. Every time I went to someone's house and saw that TV remote and all those channels, I thought, *Wow, they've got it made* — especially since my dad never allowed it in our household. It was way too expensive at the time. Fast forward to adulthood, I shared this story at an event, and someone approached me afterward to say, 'We had Foxtel, but we were broke.' Turns out, his family was financially stretched to breaking point. My mind was blown.

This story was a wake-up call: sometimes what we perceive as wealth can be a total illusion.

Social media makes it easy to fall into the trap of comparison. A while ago, I followed a fashion influencer. It looked like she had it all. She was all over Instagram with designer bags, outfits and the good life. Every outfit looked so chic, she looked like she just rolled out of bed like that. But then some of her eagle-eyed followers realised many of her luxury items were knock-offs, and the backlash was brutal.

It's a classic reminder: people can project what they want you to see while hiding the reality. The lesson is that comparing yourself to someone's social media life is like envying a movie set. It's not real! And trust me, the 'perfect' Instagram photo probably involves an Instagram boyfriend or a tripod, a filter and at least ten takes.

And let's be real: sometimes people can't even live up to their own standards, like the fashion influencer. That's why it's so important to run your own race and stay focused on your goals.

Here's the truth: seeing someone with a Lambo or a Birkin bag doesn't mean they have a lot of money. It just means they spent a lot of money — maybe money they didn't even have. Lifestyle inflation, where people spend more as they earn more, traps so many people in endless cycles of financial stress. At the end of the day, a luxury item isn't a measure of wealth; it's a measure of spending.

Neighbours of lottery winners and increased bankruptcy rates

Imagine that your neighbour wins the lottery. Suddenly, their lifestyle changes — they upgrade to a flashy new car, renovate their house and start throwing lavish parties. While you might feel happy for them, there's also a little voice in your head that starts nudging you to spend more as well. But the problem is, you didn't win the lottery.

A fascinating study by the Federal Reserve Bank of Philadelphia found that neighbours of lottery winners are significantly more likely to go bankrupt than those who don't live near a winner. This phenomenon is largely driven by 'conspicuous consumption' or the desire to visibly match the lifestyle of others around you. People see their neighbour's wealth (or what looks like wealth) and increase their own spending in response, whether or not they can actually afford it.

The study revealed that the larger the lottery prize won by a neighbour, the higher the likelihood of nearby residents experiencing financial distress. The effects were particularly pronounced for high-value lottery winnings, with neighbours often resorting to debt to fund their attempts to keep up. It's a classic case of keeping up with the Jones's!

This highlights that sometimes seeing other people with something makes us want it more. Let's say you're happily going about your day, but you see someone with the new iPhone, with all the new features and the upgraded camera. Suddenly, you start wondering whether it's time you upgraded too, but you never would have thought that unless you saw someone else with it.

What's coming up next...

In this chapter, we're flipping the script on comparison, envy and success. You'll discover:

- how to spot the illusion of wealth and why appearances can be deceiving
- the secret power of envy — and how it can guide you toward what you truly want
- why comparison is the thief of your happiness (and how to break free from it)
- how to identify your unfair advantages and use them to get ahead
- a simple gratitude practice that can shift your mindset and boost your financial confidence.

How to make envy your teacher

Here's something you might not expect: envy can actually be one of your greatest teachers. I know, it sounds counterintuitive. We're told envy is a 'bad' emotion, like it's something to feel ashamed of and ignore. But what if, instead, you leaned into it? What if envy could show you what you truly want out of life?

Let me share a story to explain what I mean.

I once had a colleague who was the kind of person who looked like she walked out of a magazine shoot every single day. You know the type: flawless lashes (always extensions, never an eyelash out of place), glowing skin, freshly manicured nails that seemed to magically regenerate every time one chipped, and outfits so immaculate you'd think she had a stylist.

Meanwhile, I'd roll into the office with my slightly wrinkled shirt, a three-day-old ponytail and nails that looked like I'd been in a scuffle with a feral animal. It wasn't just that she was stylish, it was how she made it all seem effortless.

At first, I told myself I was just annoyed by how 'extra' it all was. But, if I'm being honest, I was jealous. She wasn't just well put together; she was also one of the kindest, most genuine people I'd ever met. It was literally impossible to dislike her, she was so lovely.

That jealousy wasn't really about her, though. Once I started unpacking it, I realised it was about *me*. My shadow self (the part of me I'd repressed) was screaming, *You want to feel put together like that!* It wasn't about wanting to copy her style or spend a small fortune on nail appointments, it was about valuing the confidence that came from looking after yourself and taking pride in your appearance. What she represented was something I wanted in my own life: I wanted to feel put together and confident in my own way.

The mirror effect of envy

Envy, at its core, is like a spotlight — it doesn't just shine on what others have, it illuminates what you value or aspire to. Often, the things (or people) we envy reflect something about ourselves. They show us where we want to grow, what we admire or even what we feel we're missing.

And here's the thing: when you feel envy or jealousy creeping in, dig deeper and see where it's coming from. Most of the time, it's not the material or the surface-level things you're envying, it might be the confidence, ease or freedom those things represent. So, next time envy pops up, ask yourself these questions:

- What, specifically, am I envious of?
- Why does this make me feel this way?
- What does this reveal about my own desires or values?

Flipping envy into action

The amazing thing about envy is that it can be a tool for growth if you let it. Once you understand what your envy is telling you, use it to take action by:

- Identifying the root cause: Pinpoint what you're really envious of. Is it someone's confidence? Their career success? Their self-discipline?
- Setting personal goals: Take that envy and turn it into motivation. If you're envying someone's confidence, ask yourself what small steps you can take to build your own.
- Avoiding the comparison trap: Remember, you don't need to copy someone else's life. For me, seeing my stylish colleague didn't mean I needed her exact wardrobe, it just inspired me to take more pride in my appearance in my own way.
- Celebrating your progress: When you start working toward what you value, celebrate the small wins. Progress, not perfection, is the goal.

A new perspective on envy

Next time you feel a twinge of envy or jealousy, take a step back. Instead of spiralling into self-doubt or trying to mimic someone else's life, treat it as an opportunity for self-reflection. Maybe what you're envious of isn't their wardrobe, car or house—it might be their confidence, boldness or sense of ease.

When you lean into envy and use it as a guide, it shifts from being a negative emotion to a powerful tool for self-discovery and growth. What you envy can reveal what you truly want in life. Instead of resenting others for having it, ask yourself how you can cultivate that in your own life.

Ultimately, envy isn't something you should fear, it's something you should learn from. Let it guide you toward becoming the best version of yourself, and let the people you envy show you the way!

The role of luck in success

Success isn't just about working hard, it's also about being in the right place at the right time, avoiding major setbacks and, sometimes, just pure luck. A fascinating study titled 'Talent vs luck: The role of randomness in success and failure' simulated wealth distribution among individuals with varying levels of talent and random life events. Here's what they found—while talent was essential, the people who became *rich* rich weren't necessarily the most talented; they were the ones who worked hard and happened to avoid any major strokes of bad luck. In other words, luck didn't replace hard work, but it definitely played a role in who reached the very top.

Author Morgan Housel puts it perfectly: 'Not all success is due to hard work, and not all poverty is due to laziness.' This is something we all need to remember—being successful doesn't mean we are working the 'hardest' and there's probably some luck involved, and struggling financially doesn't mean someone isn't trying hard enough. Life isn't always a level playing field, and recognising that keeps us humble.

Reflecting on my own journey, I know I was lucky in some ways. I had access to financial education at an early age, and I was exposed to conversations about money that many people never get, thanks to my dad. That was a huge advantage. But, at the same time, I've also had to work hard, take calculated risks and make smart financial choices to get to where I am.

And here's the thing: *some things in life are just out of our control.* We can't control where we're born, the opportunities we have access to or whether a random stroke of bad luck sets us back. But what we can control is how we respond, how we manage our money and how we use the advantages we do have to move forward.

That's why, in this book, we're focusing on the Fun Finance Formula, which is all about putting our energy into the things within our control. If you remember back to Chapter 1, we talked about the top right quadrant: the *fun and skilled* money quadrant. This is where we get the best results because we're focusing on the areas where we have both ability and enjoyment. Instead of worrying about things we *can't* change, we double down on the things we *can*: learning new skills, growing our income and making our money work for us in a way that feels sustainable and fun.

The good news is we all have unfair advantages. In the next section, we'll talk about how to identify yours and use them to your advantage, because sometimes, what you think is a disadvantage can actually be your biggest strength.

Understanding your unfair advantage

Instead of comparing yourself to others, why not double down on your strengths? This is exactly what Ash Ali and Hasan Kubba discuss in their book *The Unfair Advantage*. They argue that everyone has unique, unfair advantages, which are circumstances, skills or traits that can set you apart when you learn to harness them.

Let's take Bill Gates as an example. Yes, he's one of the wealthiest people in the world, and his success is often attributed to his intelligence and hard work, but there's more to the story than meets the eye. Gates grew up with a well-off family who supported his education and interests. One of the most pivotal moments in his life came in high school, where he had access to something incredibly rare in the 1960s: a computer!

Back then, computers weren't something people had lying around or something you could pack away in a backpack. They were bulky, expensive and usually limited to universities or big corporations. But Gates's school, Lakeside School in Seattle, had a computer terminal thanks to a fundraising effort by the school's parents. While most kids his age were miles away from ever touching a computer, Gates was already programming. By the time he got to Harvard, he had years of experience under his belt — an advantage that gave him a massive head start over others when the tech revolution began.

Here's the thing: Gates still worked incredibly hard, there's no doubt about that, but he also had a head start that many didn't. His access to a computer at such a young age was an unfair advantage that allowed him to start Microsoft and, ultimately, change the world. It's a clear example of how success often isn't just about effort; luck and circumstances play a big role too. So keep this in mind next time you're comparing yourself to someone else.

But here's a twist: sometimes, what feels like a disadvantage can actually become your biggest advantage. Let me share a personal story to explain what I mean.

When I was 19, I moved out of home to live with my partner, Pablo. To say it was tough would be an understatement. In the first year, I was juggling two part-time jobs (a minimum-wage telemarketing job and a marketing internship) while studying full time at university. My weekly income was just $400, and half of that went straight to rent. That left me with only $200 to cover everything else: groceries, transport, textbooks and, well, life.

To make sure we stayed on track, Pablo and I would bring $80 in cash to the supermarket each week. It was our way of forcing ourselves not to overspend. We'd plan our meals carefully, cook dinner at home and pack leftovers for work the next day to avoid eating out. It wasn't glamorous, but it worked.

Back then, I thought I was falling behind financially. Spending so much on rent felt like a huge setback, especially when all of my friends still lived at home. But looking back now, I realise that experience was actually an advantage. Living independently taught Pablo and I how to manage our money with laser focus. We learned how to stretch every dollar, get creative and make do with what we had.

That resilience paid off in ways I never expected. I started asking for pay rises at work, taking on promotions and picking up side hustles to earn extra income. As we built up our savings, we kept many of our money-savvy habits, such as cooking at home and budgeting. Eventually, those habits gave us the foundation to save for our first home and even take overseas holidays. We found ways to travel for less by utilising credit cards and points wisely so we could book flights cheaply.

The lesson here is that sometimes, the hard things you go through — the moments that feel like setbacks — can actually make you stronger and more prepared for the future. They teach you resilience, resourcefulness and habits that set you up for long-term success. So, next time you're going through something challenging, keep this in mind because sometimes your greatest challenges can be your biggest unfair advantages.

Your turn: Reflect on your advantages

Now it's time to think about your own unfair advantages. What makes your story, your skills or your experiences unique? How can you use those to carve your own path and create opportunities for yourself? Remember, your journey doesn't need to look like anyone else's — your unfair advantages are what make it special.

Here are some examples of unfair advantages to consider:

- *Money:* Do you have savings or financial support?
- *Intelligence:* What skills, expertise or problem-solving abilities do you have?
- *Location/luck:* Are you in the right place at the right time, or have you had lucky breaks you can build on?
- *Education/experience:* What formal education or life lessons can you lean into? Do you have any professional experience you can draw from?
- *Status:* Do you have connections, a strong personal brand or a good reputation you can tap into?

Here's the thing: nobody has all of these. The key is to identify what gives you an edge and lean into it. There's no point wishing you had someone else's life — figure out what makes you unique and use it to your advantage.

Let people be successful

One thing that will change your life is realising that you've just got to let people be and let them be successful. It's so easy to dismiss someone else's achievements, to chalk them up to luck, privilege or even overspending. And while, yes, sometimes people *are* faking it or living beyond their means and some people are more privileged, as we've discussed in this chapter, there's no point in fixating on someone else's story because it only distracts you from your own journey.

What if, instead of judging or envying someone's success, we chose to celebrate it? What if we let their wins inspire us instead of making us feel smaller? It's not always easy, especially when you're grinding it out and it feels like someone else is getting ahead with half the effort. But the truth is, someone else's success doesn't take away from your potential to succeed.

And you might only be comparing your start to their middle without seeing all the challenges and obstacles they had to overcome along the way. Being happy for people's successes also allows you to be happy for your own success.

Why it's important to let people shine

Flipping the script and viewing other people's success through a positive lens is amazing for your own happiness and personal growth! Here are some reasons why.

Success leaves clues

When someone is thriving — whether it's in their career, finances or personal life — it's worth asking, *What can I learn from them?* Instead of dismissing their achievements, get curious. Did they make moves you've been afraid to take? Did they develop a skill or habit that's worth learning from? Success often leaves behind a trail of lessons and, if you're open to it, you can pick up those clues and apply them to your own life.

Judgement clouds perspective

When we judge others, we often project our insecurities on to them. Maybe you feel stuck financially, so you assume someone with a new car is irresponsible. But what if they worked hard for it, saved for years or built a business that allowed them to afford it? Constantly judging others puts you in a scarcity mindset, making it harder to focus on your own growth.

Resentment hurts you, not them

Let's be honest: feeling bitter about someone else's success doesn't hurt them — it hurts you. There's a famous quote from Buddha that says, 'Holding onto anger is like drinking poison and expecting the other person to die.' It's not worth it!

Be inspired, not intimidated

There's something powerful about flipping the script. When you see someone succeed, ask yourself:

- What did they do to get there?
- What can I learn from their journey?
- How can I use their story to motivate myself?

Let others' success light the way

At the end of the day, being happy for someone else doesn't diminish your own potential. It actually opens the door for inspiration and growth. The more we cheer each other on, the more we collectively raise the bar. So the next time you catch yourself feeling envious or dismissive of someone's success, pause and remind yourself that their win doesn't take away from yours. Let them shine, and let their light guide you toward your own success.

Practise gratitude

Sometimes I forget how lucky I am. Life gets busy, little stressful situations pile up, and suddenly I'm in full panic mode about something trivial like slow wi-fi or running out of oat milk for my coffee. But then, I take a moment to reflect on some of these mind-blowing stats and everything shifts.

Did you know that if you're eating three meals a day, you're ahead of *690 million people* who don't know when their next meal is coming? Or how about this: If you have clean drinking water at home, you're luckier than *2 billion people worldwide* who don't. Just being able to turn on a tap puts you in a privileged position.

And let's talk about safety. Around 25 per cent of the world's population — a whopping 2 billion people — live in war zones. That's one in four people facing daily threats to their lives. Meanwhile, most of us sleep peacefully at night without even thinking twice.

Even being online right now is a privilege. Nearly 37 per cent of the world's population, or about *2.9 billion people*, still don't have access to the internet. Imagine not being able to ask ChatGPT something or watch a movie on Netflix or even send an email?

When I reflect on these numbers, it's like a splash of cold water; it wakes me up to just how much I take for granted.

Building a gratitude practice

Years ago, I started a simple daily gratitude practice, and it's one of the best things I've ever done for my mindset. Every morning, I write down three things I'm grateful for. They don't have to be huge, sometimes it's as simple as 'I'm grateful to my body for keeping me alive', 'my coffee was great' or 'I had a good laugh with a friend yesterday'.

The impact has been incredible. Practising gratitude for just five minutes per day has helped me shift my focus from what I lack to what I have. It's a reminder that no matter what challenges I'm facing, there are always things to be thankful for.

Let me share a story about how gratitude saved us from what could've been a full-blown disaster. Pablo and I were returning from an amazing tropical holiday. We were cruising down the highway, feeling good and relaxed, and we could literally see the car rental drop-off in the distance — it was so close. We were five minutes away from wrapping up our trip with zero issues but, of course, life loves a little drama.

Out of nowhere—*thunk!*—we hit a pothole. And not just any pothole, we hit one that must have been hiding a sharp nail because, within seconds, we had a flat tyre. I looked at Pablo, and he looked at me, and it was that 'of course this would happen now' moment. And to make matters worse, we didn't get insurance on the rental car (which was a huge rookie mistake).

So, we pulled off the highway, got out and there we were, standing on the side of the road with a flat tyre. If this had been a year earlier, old Pablo and Queenie would've handled this very differently. Cue a blame game: 'Why did you say we didn't need to get insurance?' 'ME? It wasn't me, it was *you!*' The situation definitely would've spiralled into an argument.

But this time was different. A few months earlier, we had started practicing gratitude. So instead of pointing fingers, Pablo looked at me and said, 'Well, at least neither of us is hurt.' Then added, 'And we've had such an amazing trip. Honestly, if this is the worst thing to happen, we're pretty lucky.'

We got to work replacing the tyre and eventually made it to the car rental place. Sure, we had to pay a fee for the damage but, surprisingly, it wasn't as much as we thought it would be! In fact, it was only slightly more than what the insurance would have cost. By the time we handed over the keys, we were laughing about the whole ordeal. Honestly, the old us would've let that pothole ruin the entire day, but this time, gratitude turned a frustrating situation into just another funny travel story.

The truth is, life is full of potholes—big and small—with sharp objects inside. Things go wrong, often at the worst possible moment. But practicing gratitude helps you put things into perspective. You learn to focus on what you can control rather than what you can't control. And you focus on what's going right instead of what's going wrong. That day, I was reminded that, while we can't always control what happens, we can control how we respond. And choosing gratitude makes all the difference.

The science behind gratitude

Gratitude doesn't just make you feel good in the moment, it rewires your brain. Research shows that practicing gratitude can improve sleep, reduce stress and even increase happiness. When you start your day by focusing on the good, it sets the tone for everything else.

Let's take this study from the University of California, Davis, for example. Researchers asked participants to write down things they were grateful for every day for several weeks and measured their cortisol levels (the body's primary stress hormone). At the end of the study, participants who practiced gratitude had significantly lower cortisol levels compared with those who didn't. They also reported feeling less stressed overall. Gratitude literally calms you down, making it a simple but effective tool for reducing stress.

But it goes beyond stress — it can even rewire your brain. Researchers at Indiana University conducted a study where participants wrote gratitude letters over three weeks. Months later, brain scans showed that those who practiced gratitude had increased activity in their medial prefrontal cortex (the part of the brain responsible for learning and decision-making). This suggests that writing about gratitude can rewire your brain to make you more attuned to positive emotions.

Your turn: Try a gratitude practice for yourself

If you want to incorporate gratitude into your life, here's how you can get started:

- Keep a journal: Write down three things you're grateful for each morning. Keep it simple — even small joys count!
- Reflect during meals: Before you eat, take a moment to appreciate the food in front of you and the effort it took to get there. It's pretty amazing the things and food we have access to in this day and age; our ancestors would be very impressed!

- Pause throughout the day: When something good happens — big or small — take a moment to acknowledge it and appreciate it.

By doing this regularly, you'll start to notice how your perspective shifts. Instead of focusing on what's missing, you'll begin to see the abundance in your life. Gratitude is like a muscle: the more you use it, the stronger it gets.

So, the next time you feel like you're falling behind or focusing on what you don't have, remember: if you have food, clean water, peace and the internet, you're already incredibly fortunate — and that's something worth celebrating every day.

Key takeaways

- Wealth isn't always what it seems.
- Comparison is a trap — social media and lifestyle inflation make it easy to feel behind, but true wealth is financial freedom, not flashy spending.
- Envy can be a guide — instead of letting it bring you down, use it to identify what you truly value and take steps toward it.
- Luck plays a role in success — hard work matters, but recognising your unique unfair advantages helps you get ahead.
- Gratitude shifts everything — focusing on what you have instead of what you lack leads to greater happiness, confidence and financial peace.

In a nutshell

This chapter was all about shifting your mindset from comparison to gratitude. We explored how social media and lifestyle inflation can create an illusion of wealth, making it easy to feel like you're falling behind even when the reality is very different. The key takeaway is that wealth isn't about what you see on the surface, but about financial security and the freedom to live life on your terms.

We also uncovered the surprising power of envy and how it can actually guide you toward what you truly want. Instead of letting comparison drain your happiness, we can use it as a tool for self-reflection and motivation. Recognising your unfair advantages — whether it's your skills, experiences, or unique circumstances — allows you to lean into what makes you special, rather than trying to compete with others.

Finally, we explored the power of gratitude, backed by science, and how it can literally rewire your brain for happiness and resilience. By practising gratitude daily, you can shift your focus from what you lack to what you already have, helping you build a healthier and more confident financial mindset.

Now that you've mastered the art of choosing gratitude over comparison, the next chapter will take you through setting financial goals that truly excite you — goals that are meaningful, achievable and aligned with the life you want to create.

Chapter 4
Set GOALS that excite you

A few years ago, I decided it was time to get fit. So, like most people, I joined a gym. But it wasn't just any gym, it was one of those *hardcore* ones. You know the ones with black painted walls plastered with motivational quotes like, 'no pain, no gain'. I figured if I was going to get fit, I had to do it the 'right' way, which was... pushing through boring workouts on machines I didn't really understand, surrounded by people lifting weights twice my size.

I hated it. I'd drag myself there after work, wander around awkwardly trying to figure out the equipment, and leave feeling defeated. It was exhausting and uninspiring, and I didn't stick with it for long.

Fast forward to recently, and a friend invited me to try a pole dancing class with her. I was sceptical — wasn't pole dancing supposed to be more fun than fitness? But I went along anyway, and to my surprise, I *loved* it. From the very first class, I was hooked. The music, the energy, the vibes and the people were so supportive — it was so much fun that I didn't even realise I was working out.

I kept going back and, over time, I got stronger, more confident and actually excited about exercise. The difference was clear: when I forced myself to do something I hated, I dreaded every minute of it and I watched the clock ticking. But when I found something I genuinely enjoyed, the process became effortless and the time just flew by.

That experience taught me a powerful lesson: success doesn't come from forcing yourself to grind through something you hate. It comes from finding joy in the process. Whether it's fitness, work, or even saving money and building wealth, you're far more likely to stick with it — and thrive — when you're having fun.

What's coming up next...

This chapter is your guide to transforming your goals from a chore into something exciting and achievable. Here's what you'll learn:

- how to visualise your ideal life and then map out the steps to make it happen
- why fun goals work — when you enjoy the process, motivation comes naturally
- steps to create meaningful and fun goals
- the magic of vision boards and using visual tools to stay inspired and focused
- celebrating milestones and recognise your wins to keep the momentum going
- accountability tips to stay on track.

How to visualise your dream life

I used to think that concepts like *visualisation, manifestation* and *vision boards* were a bit woo-woo. My logic was simple: If *action* is what actually gets you there, why waste time dreaming and pinning pictures on a board? But over the years, I've realised that I was missing the point.

Imagine you get in your car, but instead of putting in a destination, you decide to wing it and just drive around. You'll probably waste a lot of time going down dead-end streets, and you don't even know where you'll end up because you haven't planned where you're going. Conversely, if you have a clear destination in mind, you can put the destination in your GPS and get there quickly.

And the same goes with having a vision of your dream life and goals you want to achieve. Having a vivid picture of what you want your life to look like can be an incredibly powerful motivator, and here's why.

Everything in your life was once just a thought

Think about it: The furniture in your home, the food in your fridge, the career you have — at one point, all of these were ideas in your head. Visualisation is simply taking your subconscious thoughts and bringing them up to the surface.

It's easier to act when you have clarity

When you have a clear vision, it's easier to work backwards and map out the steps you need to take. But if your dream is fuzzy, it's much harder to prioritise daily actions that move you forward.

You can set goals you're actually excited about

Visualisation can help you uncover what you truly desire instead of chasing goals that don't excite you. When you're excited about your vision, you're more likely to stay motivated and achieve your goals.

But first, we need to embrace this uncomfortable fact

If you're like me, you'll do anything to avoid thinking about the fact that you're going to die. We all spend a crazy amount of time avoiding thoughts about our own death, and I don't blame us — it's scary!

And it's not just us, this is deeply embedded in many cultures around the world; for example, in English, you often hear phrases like 'passed away' or 'they've gone to a better place'. All these fancy ways to avoiding saying the real words. In Spanish they say *fallecer*, which literally means 'to fail' (die). In Mandarin, they say *guò shì*, which translates to 'pass from this world'. You get the picture, we really don't want to think about death, so we even make up words and phrases so we can avoid it, because it's uncomfortable.

But, despite this discomfort, remembering that you only have one life can be one of the most powerful motivators you'll ever tap into. Confronting our own mortality forces us to look at what truly matters and to let go of the things that don't. It pushes us to use our time wisely because it's a limited resource that we'll never get back. And we never really know how long we have, or how long our loved ones have left.

So now that we're on this topic, what are you going to do with this big, beautiful, amazing life that you have? Why not use it to pursue those big, wild dreams you've been hiding away? Ultimately, you have just one life so you might as well live it on your own terms by going after what excites you most. Make your future self proud!

Your turn: The ChatGPT dream life visualisation hack

Have you ever had one of those days where everything just works and you feel fulfilled but also challenged? That's what we're about to create in this dream life visualisation exercise. So you can get clarity on what you actually want from life not what society, your parents or your past self thinks you want. We're taking it to the next level, and using ChatGPT to help you turn those thoughts into a reality.

ChatGPT will help you create a detailed vision statement that ties all your dreams together in a clear, motivating narrative. It's an exciting way to see your scattered ideas about what you would like your dream life to look and feel like transformed into something inspiring and complete.

Step 1: Imagine your ideal life ten years from now

Start by imagining yourself ten years from now. Everything has worked out for you. You're living your best life. Be specific about every detail, and allow yourself to dream big. Write down as many ideas as possible, as if you're describing your life as it is.

- If success were guaranteed, what would you achieve?
- What have you accomplished over the past decade?
- What contribution would you like to make to those around you, your community or the world?
- If you had $100 million, what would you do with your days and why?
- What childhood dreams or aspirations have you set aside but still find yourself drawn to?

Step 2: Visualisation by life area

To make this even more vivid, let's break it down into six major life areas. For each area, imagine where you want to be in ten years.

Spirituality

What is your connection with spirituality in ten years? What rituals or spiritual practices have you integrated into your life to maintain inner peace and alignment?

Health

How would you describe your physical condition in ten years? What daily habits have helped you stay in top shape?

Relationships

What do your personal and social relationships look like in ten years? What types of people make up your close circle, and how do you contribute to each others' growth?

Career

Where are you in your career in ten years? What impact have you had in your field or industry? How have you contributed to projects or initiatives that you are passionate about?

Where are you currently in your career?

Finances

What is your financial situation in ten years? What investments or strategic choices have you made to secure financial freedom for yourself and your family?

Where are you currently with your finances?

Personal development

What skills or knowledge have you developed over the past ten years that have allowed you to grow personally and professionally? What personal project or challenge have you tackled that has changed how you see yourself?

Step 3: Imagine yourself at the end of life

Now we are going to take a deep step back and reflect on what, in hindsight, would truly make you happy and proud in life. Take your time, breathe deeply and visualise this scenario vividly.

The final scene: Immersive visualisation

Close your eyes and imagine yourself in your old age, lying comfortably in a peaceful place. You are surrounded by loved ones, people with whom you've shared precious moments. You feel a deep calm, knowing your life has been rich in meaning.

- What achievements make you the proudest?
- What are the most memorable memories that come to mind?
- Who are the people you impacted most, and in what way?

Life assessment: What truly matters

Looking back, imagine you have the chance to give advice to your current self.

- What advice would you give yourself today to focus on what truly matters?
- If you had the opportunity to relive your life, what would you change to make it even more fulfilling?

Your legacy: The mark you leave

Your life is coming to an end, but the impact of your existence continues to shine. Reflect on the legacy you leave behind.

- How would you like people to remember you?
- What values, knowledge or messages do you want to pass on to future generations?
- What project or work have you left behind, and why is it so important to you?

Step 4: Write your vision statement

Now it's time to take everything you've written and turn it into a powerful vision statement: a concise, inspiring description of your ideal life.

1. Copy your answers from the previous steps.
2. Paste it into ChatGPT with this prompt:

Act as an experienced life coach who specialises in guided visualisation exercises. Your task is to craft a visualisation statement based on the following life notes. This statement should be clear, vivid and inspiring. Consider different life areas and a projection exercise focused on imagining oneself at the end of life. Incorporate details about desired possessions, goals and the envisioned future for the next ten years.

Later in this chapter, I'll show you how to convert this vision statement into structured, actionable goals.

The fun in finance

I still remember one of my birthday parties when I was a kid. We had friends over, my mum was in full 'host' mode — and my dad was nowhere to be found. Mum had sent him out hours ago to pick up sausage rolls, and we were starting to wonder if he'd gone missing for real. We were about five minutes away from forming a search party when dad finally strolled through the door, smiling from ear to ear, with some sausage rolls in his hands.

Turns out, he wasn't lost; he'd actually gone on a personal quest to find the best price. He went to three different supermarkets to compare deals. As a kid, I thought this was beyond extreme, but looking back, I see he actually *loved* doing it. Finding a bargain or a wealth-building opportunity was his favourite hobby. The same way some people chase the thrill of winning a game or buying new clothes, my dad chased the thrill of saving money.

That passion definitely rubbed off on me. These days, I get a little jolt of excitement if I can snag the same item cheaper somewhere else — or better yet, combine a price match with a coupon code and a cash back app. That's why it takes me at least 30 minutes to actually buy something online. I'm equally obsessed with automating my savings, using offset accounts to slice down my mortgage interest rate, and automating my investments so my money can quietly multiply in the background while I enjoy my life.

And that's exactly how you can approach your financial goals: as a *fun* game, rather than a chore. Whether it's finding the best deals, trimming down your mortgage interest or automating your investments, it can be something you *look forward to* — just like my dad turned a simple errand into a treasure hunt for the ultimate discount. After all, isn't it more exciting to see how your wealth can grow when you're *enjoying* the process?

Here are some ways to create fun financial goals you're actually excited about.

Turn your finances into a game

According to a study by Patel et al., adding game-like elements such as rewards and leaderboards dramatically increases motivation and sustained engagement. You can apply this to money in a number of ways.

Creating money competitions

Set up competitions for yourself around saving or investing money; for example, saving your first $10 000 or $100 000. I personally love to track my net worth every month. Your net worth is the value of your assets minus your liabilities. Assets include your stock portfolio, superannuation and home value, while liabilities are things like your mortgage, student loans and credit card debt. Watching my net worth increase over time is like finding out my favourite TV show has dropped a new episode for me to watch on Netflix!

Milestone rewards

Give yourself small treats for each saving or investing milestone. For example, for every $1000 saved, you get to spend $100 guilt-free on whatever you like. I personally love going out for little treats like a beautiful pastry, gelato or bubble tea. I love how these treats are inexpensive, but they're so much fun. It also means I can stretch my $100 even further.

Treat yourself with unexpected money wins

Let's say you sold something on Facebook Marketplace that you don't use anymore. You can save 50 per cent and spend 50 per cent on something you love (we talk more about the save some, spend some strategy in Chapter 7). I personally did this with a camera I no longer used, and I did the math: selling that item bought me one bubble tea a week for ages.

Progress trackers

Use a spreadsheet or a budgeting tool like Billroo, developed by me and available at billroo.com, so that you can visually see where your money is going. Watching the numbers grow can be surprisingly addictive — and fun!

Richard Branson is a perfect example of turning his business into a game. From launching airlines to space travel, Branson thrives on excitement and fun. He even once said, 'If you're not having fun, you're doing it wrong.'

When you view challenges as fun rather than stressful, you stay motivated and resilient, traits that have helped Branson build a multi-billion-dollar empire.

Get into the 'flow' state

Psychologist Mihaly Csikszentmihalyi introduced the concept of flow in his book *Flow: The psychology of optimal experience*. Flow occurs when you're deeply immersed in an activity that balances challenge and skill, creating a sense of enjoyment and focus. This is exactly what we were talking about in Chapter 1, when we focused on the top right quadrant, which is fun and skilled money (money that is within your control). Here's how to tap into your flow state when it comes to your finances.

Make it slightly challenging, but not too much too fast

If you're new to budgeting, start simple (for example, track expenses weekly with a tool like Billroo or in a spreadsheet). As your skills grow, challenge yourself with more complex tasks such as investing or starting a side hustle. Focus on the things you can control in the fun and skilled money quadrant.

Set a regular time to check in on your finances

Schedule a dedicated 'money hour' once a week or once a month to review your finances. I personally do this every month. I go through my expenses and see where my money went, and then make a plan for the next month. Put your phone on silent and turn off notifications so you can really let yourself get absorbed in the process.

Beyoncé is a perfect example of flow. She's described performing as her happy place. When she's on stage, she enters a state of flow, where everything just clicks. This intense passion for performing keeps her going, even during gruelling rehearsals and world tours.

Doing what you love creates a flow state, making hard work feel effortless. If your goals excite you, you'll push through the tough moments.

Embrace learning and growth

A meta-analysis by Sailer et al. found that 'gamified' educational experiences led to higher engagement, deeper learning and better long-term retention. Here's how you can do the same for your money goals:

- Level up your knowledge: Allow yourself to consume personal finance content and learn new skills so you can feel like you're levelling up in a game. Each new strategy or concept mastered is like capturing a Pokémon!

- Celebrate small wins: Each time you master a new money skill, give yourself a micro-reward — whether it's a fancy coffee or going for a nice walk with a friend.

Make your goals your own

Back in high school, I attended one of those super-competitive selective schools — you know, the kind where everyone's tackling advanced math problems and actually enjoying it. Meanwhile, I was quietly panicking over equations that looked like rocket science. But because I'd bought into the idea that the 'real smart kids' took advanced math, I stuck with it, even though I spent most of class trying not to ask questions that felt, let's be honest, pretty dumb.

Eventually, I hit my breaking point. When it came time to choose electives, I dropped advanced math for general math, which was easier and actually *useful* for real life (who would've thought?). I also signed up for art, even though it wasn't considered a 'smart' subject. And the result was incredible. I *loved* my classes *and* I aced my exams. I still got into the tough university course I wanted, and (here's the real deal) I actually enjoyed studying — I know, I'm as surprised as you are! And it's all because I was learning things I genuinely cared about.

That lesson carried over to my finances later on. I realised you can't build money habits you hate and expect to stick with them. You've got to choose goals that excite you. For me, that means prioritising travel in my budget (it's my happy place), which I balance out by trimming my eating-out category. I love clothes, but I don't chase every trend. I'd rather invest in timeless pieces I'll wear again and again, as part of my capsule wardrobe (which we'll talk about in Chapter 5) instead of impulse-buying trendy outfits that I'll only wear for a season.

Pablo and I also prioritised buying our first home versus spending money on a lavish wedding — although, power to you, if that's one of your goals. Personal finances are personal, and I totally understand that for some people and some cultures this is expected. We just decided that we'd prefer to invest our money into buying a home first.

The results of this are that I've found a system that works for me, because I actually find it fun. I track my expenses each month, set savings targets and chart my net worth. Watching that net worth number increase over time is like watching your favourite athlete winning a game — and that's exactly how I stay motivated.

So the moral of the story is: don't pick financial goals because they look 'smart' or impress other people. Pick the ones that light you up inside, because when you genuinely enjoy the process, you'll be a whole lot more likely to stick with it — and actually succeed!

Your turn: How to turn your dream life vision into actionable goals

Ever wish you had a roadmap to achieving your dream life? Well, now I'm going to show you how you can take your dream life visualisation that we did back on page 61 and break it down into steps to make it happen. And don't worry, I've got a fun, super-efficient ChatGPT trick that can help you do it in minutes.

Step 1: Convert your vision into goals

We're going to turn that vision you came up with during the visualisation exercise into OKRs, which is basically a structured way of creating *actionable* goals. By translating your daydreams into measurable steps, you'll have a clear roadmap to follow.

All you have to do is copy and paste your dream life visualisation into ChatGPT with the following prompt:

> *Act as a strategic planner specialising in long-term vision and goal-setting. Break down a ten-year vision into OKRs for three years, one year, and three months organised by the following life*

> areas: career, finance, health/physical, personal/educational, relational and spiritual. Pay special attention to the career and finance areas. Clearly define objectives to set the direction and measurable key results to mark progress.

ChatGPT will then generate a detailed plan of OKRs for each timeframe across every important area of your life. In just a few minutes, you'll have a clear set of steps to start moving toward the future you've envisioned!

Step 2: Convert your OKRs into projects, tasks and habits

But we're not done yet. Use this next ChatGPT prompt to turn those OKRs into habits, so you know the habits you'll need to adopt in order to get to your dream life. In other words, you'll be able to see exactly what you need to do (and when) to make your dream life a reality.

> Act as a strategic operations manager and organise a three-year, one-year and three-month OKR plan into actionable steps. Structure these actions as projects or habits. For each project, list clear, precise tasks to follow. Assign deadlines for each project and estimate the time required for each task or habit.

This ChatGPT prompt will break down your three-year, one-year and three-month OKRs into specific projects and daily/weekly habits. This will give you a clear roadmap of tasks and deadlines so you know exactly how to move forward. By turning high-level goals into concrete actions (complete with timelines and task breakdowns), you'll always know your next step on the path to your ideal future.

Step 3: Commit to your dream life

Now that you have:

- created a clear vision of your dream life
- defined your long-term goals across key life areas
- translated them into measurable objectives and key results
- developed an action plan to start moving forward...

...the real work begins. It's important to check in with your vision statement regularly and read it daily or weekly to stay inspired.

Don't forget to celebrate your progress and small wins along the way. Every step forward is progress. You can always adjust it as you go. Life is constantly changing, and your vision can change too.

This isn't just a dream — it can be your future. Now you have the roadmap to make it happen. You just need to take action so you can turn those thoughts into a reality.

Accountability tips

Setting financial goals is one thing — actually achieving them is another. While motivation can get you started, accountability is what keeps you going. Research shows that when people commit to their goals publicly and check in regularly with an accountability partner, their chances of success skyrocket.

So how can you apply this principle to your own finances? Here are a few ways.

Find an accountability partner

Whether it's a friend, a partner or a financial coach, having someone to check in with regularly can keep you on track and make the process more fun. Some ways to do this:

- Money check-ins: Set a monthly or quarterly call with a friend where you both review your savings, investment progress or debt payoff.
- Friendly challenges: Compete on goals like 'who can save the most in three months' or 'who can go a week without impulse purchases'.
- Public commitment: If you're comfortable, share your goals with a small group or online community to boost accountability.

Track and report your progress

Even if you don't have an accountability buddy, self-accountability works too. Try:

- Monthly expense reviews: Log your spending and reflect on what worked.
- Net worth tracking: Watching your assets grow over time is super motivating!
- Automated updates: Set calendar reminders for personal finance check-ins.

Make it official: Write it down

One of the most powerful strategies is to write down your financial goals and break them into smaller, trackable steps; for example, instead of saying, 'I want to save $10 000 this year', write:

- Goal: Save $10 000 in 12 months
- Plan: Save $833/month → $208/week

- Deadline: Review progress at the end of each month
- Check-in: Share your progress with an accountability partner.

The key to financial success isn't just setting goals, it's about consistently working toward them. Find a way to add accountability into your money journey, whether that's through a friend, a coach or even tracking tools. When you know someone (even future *you*) is watching, you're far more likely to take action and actually reach your financial goals.

Key takeaways

- Joy fuels success: You're more likely to stick with your goals when the process is fun, not forced.
- Visualisation = Clarity: A clear vision of your dream life helps you map out the steps to get there.
- Your time is limited — use it wisely: Embracing the reality of life's impermanence can be the ultimate motivator.
- Gamify your goals: Turning your financial journey into a game makes saving, investing and budgeting exciting.
- Find your flow: Align your money habits with activities you enjoy to stay consistent without burnout.
- Small wins matter: Celebrate milestones along the way — progress keeps you motivated.
- Accountability is your secret weapon: Sharing your goals with someone (or even future you) increases the chance you'll achieve them.

In a nutshell

Whether it's fitness, saving money or achieving a career milestone, the secret isn't just hard work — it's finding joy in the process. Like my journey from awkward gym sessions to fun pole-dancing classes, the path to success becomes so much easier when you're doing something you love.

In this chapter, we've unlocked a new step in the Fun Finance Formula: Create goals that excite you! When your goals light you up inside, staying motivated feels effortless. It's not about grinding through tasks — it's about building a life that excites you every step of the way.

Now that you've set goals that inspire you, it's time for the next step in the formula: Spending with intention. In the next chapter, we'll explore how to align your spending with what truly matters to you, so every dollar moves you closer to the life you've dreamed of.

Chapter 5

Spend with INTENTION

You've probably heard the saying 'money can't buy happiness', and in some ways, that's true. You can't tap your card and suddenly feel fulfilled. You can't purchase deep, meaningful friendships or a lifetime of happy memories. But what if I told you that how you spend your money can directly impact your happiness?

The truth is, you can spend money on anything, but you can't spend it on everything. This means making choices about where your money goes, and aligning them with your values and goals. Whether it's travel, hobbies or investing in quality items, the key is to prioritise what brings you the most happiness and let go of the rest.

> ### What's coming up next...
>
> In this chapter, we're diving into how to spend your money with purpose and joy. You'll learn:
>
> - what actually makes people happy (according to science)
> - how to spend with intention, so every dollar aligns with your values
> - why experiences beat possessions when it comes to lasting happiness
> - why spending more can sometimes save you money
> - how giving to others can boost your own happiness.
>
> Get ready to transform the way you spend because money isn't just for saving, it's for living.

What actually makes us happy?

For over 85 years, Harvard researchers have been studying what truly makes people happy. Their findings are clear: the biggest factor in long-term happiness isn't wealth, fame or success — it's the quality of our relationships.

The Harvard Happiness Study is one of the longest-running research projects on happiness. The study followed participants from all walks of life: college students, factory workers, doctors and even US presidents. Decades later, when these people reflected on their lives, it wasn't their careers, bank balances or the big fancy home they owned that stood out — it was the relationships they built and the experiences they shared.

One participant, a successful businessman, shared that even though he had amassed significant wealth, his happiest memories were not of his financial achievements but about road-tripping with his family when his kids were young. Another participant, a former factory worker, said the best moments of his life were simply Sunday lunches with close friends.

This study proves that deep social connections are the key to lasting happiness. But while money can't buy stronger relationships, it can facilitate experiences that bring people together: trips with loved ones, shared meals, concerts and adventures that become the stories we tell for years.

What makes people happier over time?

While relationships are the most important factor contributing to happiness, research also shows that how we spend our money directly affects how happy we feel over time.

Dr Gilovich and his team at Cornell conducted a series of studies where they asked people about their purchases: some had spent money on material possessions (e.g., electronics, clothes or furniture), while others had spent money on experiences (e.g., trips, concerts or outdoor adventures).

Participants were asked how happy they felt immediately after the purchase and then again months and years later.

At first, both groups reported similar levels of happiness. Whether it was a new phone or a dream vacation, everyone felt that rush of excitement, but over time, a clear difference emerged.

- People who bought material possessions adapted to them quickly. The excitement faded as they got used to their new items.
- People who spent money on experiences reported that their happiness actually grew over time.

Even when experiences weren't perfect, such as a rainy holiday or a concert where they lost their voice from screaming too much, people still remembered them fondly. And the reason why is because experiences don't just make us happy in the moment, they become part of our identity.

How to buy happiness

This research led to a powerful discovery: if you want to 'buy' happiness, spend it on experiences, not just things.

That doesn't mean material things are bad — far from it. Some purchases (like a great pair of boots or a high-quality laptop) can absolutely bring value to your life, but if you want to maximise happiness, prioritise experiences that create memories, deepen relationships and become part of your story and your identity. At the end of the day, you won't treasure every gadget you buy, but you will cherish the memories you make with the people you love.

The surprising reason we get used to the 'things' in our life

In 1978, psychologists Philip Brickman, Dan Coates and Ronnie Janoff-Bulman conducted one of the most eye-opening studies on happiness. They compared two groups: lottery winners and paraplegics.

At first, the results were predictable: lottery winners reported a huge spike in happiness after winning, while paraplegics experienced a steep decline after their life-changing accident.

But here's where it gets shocking: One year later, both groups had returned to their baseline level of happiness.

The lottery winners had adapted to their wealth, and the joy of buying new cars, clothes and houses had faded. Meanwhile, the paraplegics, despite their challenges, found ways to build meaning in their lives — strengthening relationships, finding new hobbies and gaining a renewed appreciation for life.

This study demonstrates the hedonic adaptation effect: we quickly adjust to new circumstances, whether positive or negative. Material purchases don't bring lasting happiness because we get used to them, but experiences keep giving because they become part of our identity. Our experiences shape how we see the world and ourselves.

Experiences also connect us with other people. When you buy a new gadget, it's mostly for you. When you go on a trip, see a live performance or even take a cooking class, it's something that connects you with other people.

The Uluru trip that turned into a comedy special

Picture this: A couple on a budget, an $80 tent and the wettest week in Uluru's recorded history. What could possibly go wrong? (Spoiler alert: Everything.)

Pablo and I had always wanted to visit Uluru, one of Australia's most iconic landmarks. We found some super cheap flights and thought, this is it — bucket list moment! It was the Christmas holidays, which, if you live in Australia, you know means heat. Lots of heat. And Uluru, smack-bang in the middle of the country, is basically Mars: red earth, tiny shrubs and a whole lot of sun.

When we landed, it was breathtaking. The landscape was unlike anything we had ever seen. It felt like stepping onto another planet. But along with the beauty came the flies. I'm not talking about a few annoying little bugs, I mean more than I've ever experienced in my life. Massive flies that, for some reason, were obsessed with attacking our eyes. We quickly learned that fly nets weren't just an optional accessory, they were a necessity for survival.

Now, here's where our budget-savvy brilliance came into play. There were three accommodation options:

1. fancy resort with a pool and air conditioning
2. midrange hotel with actual walls and a roof
3. camping.

Since we were in our frugal era, we went for option three: bring our own tent and camp. What could go wrong? Oh, just the fact that we unknowingly booked our trip during the wettest period in Uluru's recorded history.

The unexpectedly rainy Uluru trip

We arrived, set up our cheap, flimsy tent and, just as we were patting ourselves on the back for our smart financial decision, the heavens opened. And not just any light drizzle — it was torrential rain. The kind that makes you question all of your life choices.

It rained nonstop. The driest place in Australia had turned into a giant red mud puddle. The campsite was flooded, and within 24 hours, we were the only ones left. Every other camper had abandoned ship and upgraded to actual accommodation. But not us. Oh no, we were too committed (and too broke) to leave.

There were giant, ankle-deep puddles everywhere, so walking to the shower was like a puddle minefield. And each night we wondered whether we'd wake up floating down a newly formed Uluru river.

To make things worse, we couldn't even cook because, you know, fire and water don't mix. So we took the free shuttle bus to the town supermarket, where we bought the finest gourmet meals one can cook in a camping station microwave. We feasted on two-minute noodles and microwave mac and cheese. We huddled under a small shelter at the campsite, eating our steaming bowls of instant sadness, while watching the rain mock us.

At this point, we were questioning everything. Why did we think this was a good idea? Why did we trust an $80 tent to protect us from the wrath of nature? Why didn't we just stay home and watch Netflix?

But then, the magic moments happed

As much as we were miserable in the moment, Uluru still gave us some of the most incredible experiences of our lives.

Since we had saved money on accommodation (which, let's be real, was a mistake), we had extra money to splurge on amazing experiences, such as taking a small plane ride over Uluru. Seeing the vastness of the desert from above was unreal. We explored sacred sites and learned about Indigenous culture. Their stories and artwork were unlike anything we had ever seen. We ate dinner under the stars — with no city lights around, the sky was so clear we could see entire galaxies and the Milky Way stretched across the sky.

And despite all the chaos, those were the moments we remembered the most.

Why mishaps make the best memories

Looking back, the rain-soaked disaster that was our Uluru trip is now one of our favourite stories. It was awful, but it was also hilarious. And that's the funny thing about life — even the moments that feel terrible at the time can become the best memories.

Psychologists call this the endowed progress effect — the idea that we look back on experiences more fondly over time, even if things didn't go to plan.

- Think about a holiday where everything went perfectly. It was probably amazing, but do you talk about it often?
- Now think about a time when things went a little (or very) wrong. Those are the stories you tell over and over.

It's why people love reminiscing about missed flights, language mishaps or unexpected adventures. They become part of your life's highlight reel.

Find what brings you joy

Now, this isn't to say that material things don't have value. If buying a designer bag, a dream car or a luxury watch represents a milestone for you — that's amazing! Money should be spent on things that genuinely make you happy.

The key takeaway is to be intentional with your spending. Whether it's experiences, milestone purchases, or a mix of both, make sure your money is creating value in your life in a way that feels meaningful to you. For me, spending money on experiences has been one of the best investments in happiness, but what matters most is finding what makes you feel fulfilled.

At the end of the day, happiness isn't about how much money you have, it's about how you use it. So whether it's travel, experiences, beautiful items or all of the above, spend in a way that makes your life richer — not just in wealth, but in memories, meaning and happiness.

How to be more intentional with gifts

One of my favourite things about Pablo is how intentional and thoughtful he is when it comes to giving gifts — not just to me, but to everyone around him. He has this uncanny ability to know exactly what someone needs, sometimes before they even realise it themselves.

For example, if I casually mention that I'm running low on my favourite sunscreen, Pablo will quietly make a mental note. If I have an event coming up and need something specific, he somehow just knows. And when my birthday, Christmas or Valentine's Day rolls around, I'm always amazed at how he gets it right every single time.

But what really struck me was that this wasn't just something he did for me, it was how he approached giving in general.

One of my favourite examples of how a small, thoughtful gift can have a lasting impact happened when we visited Pablo's family in France for Christmas.

Pablo was raised by a single mum who worked incredibly hard as a self-employed flute repairer in Paris. While they always had enough for what they needed, they were mindful of how they spent their money. Growing up, Pablo learned that a thoughtful gift didn't have to be expensive, it just had to be meaningful.

One night, while we were having dinner, I was talking with Pablo's aunt about Christmas gifts, and I casually mentioned how thoughtful Pablo was when it came to gift-giving. She smiled and said, 'Oh, he really is. There's one gift he gave me years ago that I still use every single day. Every time I see it, I think of him.'

She told me about how she had gotten a new coffee machine but didn't have a proper stand to organise her coffee pods. Pablo, remembering her mentioning it in passing, bought her a little stand to hold all her coffee pods.

It was such a simple, inexpensive gift, but because it was something she actually needed and used daily, it became one of her favourite gifts of all time.

And that's the thing about thoughtful giving: it doesn't have to be grand, expensive or extravagant. The best gifts are often the ones that quietly improve someone's life in a small but meaningful way. And if you plan your gifts in advance, you can take advantage of sales and discounts instead of scrambling last minute and getting it a full price.

I noticed that, throughout the year, Pablo was always listening. If family or friends mentioned they needed something, he would store it away in his memory so that when it was time to buy a gift, he wasn't scrambling for a last-minute candle or a box of chocolates. He'd already thought about it.

Seeing this inspired me to change my own approach to gift-giving. I used to just buy people generic, impersonal gifts like candles, a bottle of wine or a box of chocolates. Nothing wrong with those, but let's be real, most of the time, they're just a safe option, not something meaningful.

But now, I do what Pablo does. I keep a mental (and sometimes physical) list throughout the year of what people mention they need or want. When Christmas or birthdays come around, I already know exactly what to get them — something that's useful, meaningful and genuinely makes their life better.

And it turns out, there's actual science behind why this kind of generosity makes us happier.

The science of giving

In 2008, researchers Elizabeth Dunn, Lara Aknin and Michael Norton at the University of British Columbia put generosity to the test in one of the most fascinating studies on happiness. They gave random people either $5 or $20 and told them to spend it before the end of the day. Half the participants were told to spend the money on themselves, buying coffee, snacks or something small. The other half had to spend it on someone else: a friend, a stranger or a donation.

At the end of the day, the researchers checked in and asked: Who felt happier?

It turns out, the amount of money didn't matter. Whether they got $5 or $20, the participants who spent their money on others reported significantly higher levels of happiness than those who spent it on themselves.

Even a small act of generosity (like covering a friend's coffee) brought more joy than buying something for themselves, and it turns out, generosity is contagious.

How kindness creates a ripple effect

In 2014, a Starbucks drive-thru in Florida had a chain reaction of generosity. One customer bought a coffee for the person behind them, and that act of generosity created a ripple effect that lasted 11 hours, covering over 378 customers.

Why did this happen? Because generosity is contagious. When someone experiences an act of kindness, like someone before them buying them a coffee, they feel an urge to pay it forward, spreading happiness far beyond the original giver.

This is something I've experienced first-hand.

By watching Pablo's intentional gift-giving, I started doing the same — and it changed the way I thought about generosity.

Why giving feels good

There's a reason why giving gifts feels just as good (if not better) than receiving them. When you give a meaningful gift, it's not just the recipient who experiences joy — you do too.

Studies show that generosity activates the brain's reward system, releasing dopamine, the same chemical responsible for feelings of happiness and pleasure. That's why giving actually makes us feel so good!

And the joy of giving isn't just in the moment; it lingers.

- When you pick out the gift, you feel excited about how the person will react.
- When you give it to them, you feel happy watching their joy.
- Every time they use it, they think of you — and that memory makes them smile again, just like Pablo's aunt!

In a way, giving is like a happiness investment: it keeps paying off long after the moment has passed.

Be intentional with your giving

If you're going to spend money on gifts anyway, why not make it count? Instead of rushing out at the last minute to buy a generic present, try this:

- Listen throughout the year: Pay attention when people mention something they want or need.
- Keep a list: Jot the idea down in your phone so you don't forget.
- Be thoughtful, not flashy: The best gifts aren't the most expensive, they're the most meaningful.

How spending more upfront can (sometimes) save you money

A few years ago, Pablo and I decided we wanted to buy a beach cabana. You know, one of those big beach shelters that's perfect for summer. The thing is, they're not cheap — they cost around $189, which felt like a lot of money for something we weren't sure we'd use heaps. So, naturally, we decided to look for a cheaper option.

Sure enough, we found one for about $80, significantly less than the original we were eyeing. It looked decent enough online, so we bought it, feeling pretty smug about saving money. But the first time we used it at the beach, oh my god, was a disaster. The cabana was made of flimsy material and lightweight plastic, and it couldn't handle even a mildly windy day. While everyone else's OG cabanas stood strong, ours wobbled like a newborn giraffe. Then, to make matters worse, we accidentally tore a hole in the fabric on its very first outing.

After just two uses, we had to throw it away. That $80 was essentially wasted. The cost per use? A staggering $40 per outing. Ouch.

Eventually, we bit the bullet and bought the original cabana we were eyeing. We managed to get it slightly cheaper on sale, but even if we hadn't, the $189 would've been worth every cent. The OG cabana is made from durable steel and sturdy fabric, and even on windy days, it doesn't budge. We've now had it for three years and use it at least 20 times every summer. The cost per use so far? Less than $3 — and it's still going strong!

The lesson was crystal clear: sometimes spending more upfront can save you money (and headaches) in the long run.

The cost-per-use formula

Here's a simple formula to help you decide if something is worth the price: the cost-per-use formula.

Let's look at the OG cabana we bought. The cabana cost $189, and we've used it 20 times every summer for three years: 60 uses in total. Therefore, the cost per use is just $3.15. Compare that to the $80 cabana we bought first, which only lasted two outings, costing us $40 per use.

This formula helps you think beyond the price of the item and focus on its long-term value. It's not about buying cheap, it's about buying smart.

The science of cost per use

Now, I know what you're probably thinking: 'Queenie, are you just gaslighting me into spending more money?' Or maybe, 'Isn't cost-per-use just some suspicious shopping math we tell ourselves to justify buying expensive things?'

Fair questions. But science actually backs this up. Research has shown that spending a little more upfront can actually save you money in the long run — if you do it right. Let me explain.

Short-term savings vs long-term impact?

Now, you'd think that when faced with two options (one cheap but low-quality, the other expensive but long-lasting) people would naturally choose the one that saves them money in the long run, right?

Nope!

In a 2009 study by Shane Frederick, Nathan Novemsky and Nobel Prize-winning psychologist Daniel Kahneman, researchers found that most people still go for the cheaper option, even when they *know* the expensive one will last longer.

This is because our brains are wired to feel the pain of spending money immediately rather than thinking about long-term value. This is known as myopic loss aversion, where we focus too much on short-term savings instead of long-term financial impact.

It's why people hesitate to spend $200 on a durable jacket that lasts ten years but will happily spend $50 on a trendy one that falls apart after one winter.

The problem is that the 'cheap' jacket ends up costing $500 over a decade ($50 x 10), while the 'expensive' jacket only costs $200. Sometimes, the cheaper option is the most expensive decision you can make.

But that's not all: the environmental impact of fast fashion is massive.

The fast fashion problem

We're buying more clothes than ever — and throwing them away just as fast.

In the US, the average American buys 68 pieces of new clothing every year and throws away 37 kilograms of clothing annually. That's over 11.3 million tons of textile waste heading to landfill each year.

Australians buy 56 items of new clothing per year, one of the highest rates globally, and discard 23 kilograms of clothing per person annually, with 260 000 tonnes of clothes ending up in landfill every year.

Consider a capsule wardrobe

Instead of buying 56+ new items per year, what if we flipped the script and we invested in fewer, higher-quality pieces that last years instead of months?

This is where a capsule wardrobe comes in: a game-changer for anyone who wants to look stylish while spending less and reducing waste.

A capsule wardrobe is a curated collection of versatile, high-quality clothing items that can be mixed and matched to create dozens of different outfits. The beauty of this approach? You don't need hundreds of pieces to have endless outfit options, you just need the right pieces.

Think about it, instead of:

- ten pairs of trendy jeans that go out of style, you own two or three high-quality pairs that fit perfectly and last for years
- 20 fast fashion tops that fall apart after a few washes, you have four to six timeless tops that go with everything
- impulse-buying random items that don't match, you create a wardrobe where nearly everything works together.

The key to an effortless capsule wardrobe is balance:

- 80 per cent neutral colours (think black, white, beige, tan, navy): these are your basics that go with everything
- 20 per cent colours or statement pieces: pops of colour, prints or fun accessories that make your outfits feel fresh and personal.

(And if you're someone who loves colour, you can totally create a colourful capsule wardrobe instead; just stick to a complementary colour palette so your pieces mix and match easily!)

How to create 100+ outfits with just 13 pieces

Did you know that just 13 essential pieces can create over 100 different outfits? Here's a simple breakdown:

- 4 tops
- 4 bottoms
- 1 dress
- 2 outerwear
- 2 pairs of shoes

How the combinations work:

- Without outerwear: 4 tops × 4 bottoms × 2 shoes = 32 outfits
- With outerwear: 4 tops × 4 bottoms × 2 outerwear × 2 shoes = 64 outfits
- 1 dress + 2 shoes = 2 outfits
- 1 dress + 2 outerwear + 2 shoes = 4 outfits

Total combinations = 102 outfits from just 13 pieces!

If 13 sounds too few, you do you! You could even create a different capsule for each season.

The big takeaway for me is that you actually don't need that many items of clothing in order to create a variety of different looks! So that's why I think it makes sense to invest in high-quality, timeless pieces you can wear again and again. It's good for our finances, better for the planet and it feels good to wear high-quality pieces we love too.

How a capsule wardrobe can save you money

Let's compare and see how spending more on a quality item that lasts longer can actually cost you less overall. Let's compare:

Fast fashion:

- 10 tops at $30 each = $300
- Worn 3 times each = $10 per wear

Capsule wardrobe approach:

- 4 high-quality tops at $75 each = $300
- Worn 50+ times each = $1.50 per wear

Important: Not all expensive things are 'worth it'

Now, let's be clear — I'm not saying that buying the most expensive item is always worth it. And I'm definitely not saying that you should never buy cheap products.

Not all expensive items are worth the price. Price doesn't always equal quality.

There are plenty of overpriced things that aren't any better than the cheaper option, and, sometimes, buying the budget-friendly option is the better move.

What I am saying is that it's important to consider the long-term cost per use of an item before making a purchase. If it's something you'll use often, if it aligns with your style or needs, or if it genuinely makes you happy, then it's worth considering the long-term cost per use.

At the end of the day, money isn't just about what you spend — it's about what you get in return.

Things to consider before you make a purchase

Before you go out and justify every luxury purchase by yelling 'cost per use!', let's go through some things to really consider before you make a purchase.

Ask yourself these questions before buying something:

- Will this last a long time, or will I need to replace it soon?
- Will I actually use it often enough to justify the cost?

- Is the cheaper option really a bargain, or will I have to replace it three times?
- Am I just trying to talk myself into an unnecessary purchase? (Be honest.)

If it checks out, spending more upfront might actually be the smarter financial move.

Spending with intention

We often think about money in terms of how much we earn or save, but the real magic happens when we focus on how we spend. It's not about spending less, it's about spending on what actually makes us happy.

Have you ever looked at your bank statement and thought, *Where did all my money go?* Or worse, felt a pang of regret over something you bought that didn't bring you as much joy as you expected? (This is heavy money showing up again, as we discussed in Chapter 1.) If so, you're not alone.

But the good news is we can change that.

By taking an intentional approach to spending, we can ensure that our hard-earned money goes toward things that truly light us up, instead of being mindlessly drained away on things that don't.

How we spend with intention

Every month, Pablo and I sit down and review our expenses — not in a restrictive kind of way; more like detectives solving the mystery of where our money went.

We go through our transactions, not to shame ourselves, but to learn from our spending patterns.

- Did our money go toward things that genuinely made us happy?

- Were there any purchases we regretted?
- Are there areas where we could shift our spending to bring us more joy?

For example, at the end of 2024, we realised that travel had been one of our biggest sources of happiness, but we hadn't done as much of it as we wanted. For the next year, we made a decision to prioritise travel, setting aside 15 per cent of our income for it.

Of course, this meant we had to cut back in other areas. We made some intentional trade-offs:

- reduced our dining-out budget
- scaled back on clothing purchases
- became more mindful of grocery spending.

And you know what? We never felt deprived because we were still spending on what we valued most. This is what spending with intention is all about: funnelling your money toward the things that bring you real happiness.

Your turn: Discover where your money goes

This is one of my favourite money exercises — and it's actually fun! It's time to solve your own money mystery.

Step 1: Gather your spending data

Start by downloading your transactions from the last three months. You can download them from your bank's online portal, use a budgeting tool such as Billroo to categorise them automatically or export them into an Excel spreadsheet and sort through them manually.

Step 2: Categorise your spending

Look at where your money has gone and place each transaction into one of these four categories:

- Loved it! This was money well spent. It brought me joy or was truly useful (fun money).
- Meh… It was fine, but I wouldn't be sad if I didn't buy it again (heavy money).
- Regret it. This was a waste of money. I wish I'd spent it on something else (still heavy money).
- Essential expenses. Rent, bills, groceries — things that aren't exciting but necessary.

Step 3: Find your spending patterns

Once you've sorted everything, ask yourself these questions:

- What purchases brought you the most happiness?
- Are there any surprising purchases you regret?
- Where can you reallocate money from the 'meh' or 'regret' categories into things you love?

Step 4: Align your spending with your values

Now that you know where your money is going, let's make it work for you.

- List your top three priorities for the next year (e.g., travel, investing, health).
- Look at your spending and make sure it reflects those priorities.
- Adjust your budget to cut back on things that don't bring you joy and increase spending in areas that do.

Spending with intention is spending with happiness

The goal of spending with intention isn't to spend as little as possible, it's to make sure every dollar you spend aligns with what you truly value.

When you look back at your spending at the end of the year, imagine being able to say:

- I don't regret a single dollar I spent.
- Every purchase added value to my life.
- I spent money on things that made me truly happy.

That's the real power of intentional spending. So, next time you're about to make a purchase, ask yourself:

- Is this truly adding value to my life?
- Does it align with my goals and priorities?
- Will I look back and be happy I spent this money?

If the answer is 'yes', go for it. If not, maybe redirect those funds to something that brings you more happiness. At the end of the day, money is just a tool, and the best way to use it is to build a life you love.

Key takeaways

- Money can buy happiness — if you spend it right.
- Intentional spending = financial freedom: Align your spending with your values to make every dollar count.
- Cost per use is your secret weapon: Sometimes spending more upfront saves you money in the long run.
- Generosity feels good (and is science-backed): Giving to others can boost your own happiness.
- Review, reflect, reallocate: Regularly check your spending to ensure it's bringing you closer to the life you want.

In a nutshell

When you spend intentionally, money becomes more than just numbers, it becomes a tool to create memories, support your values and build a life you love. It's not about cutting back; it's about spending smarter on what truly matters to you.

Now you've unlocked this step in the Fun Finance Formula: spending with intention. In the next chapter, we'll dive into the 3Fs of Budgeting: foundation, fun and freedom, where you'll learn how to create a budget that balances security with spontaneity, so your money works for you. Let's go!

Chapter 6
BALANCE the 3Fs: Foundation, fun and freedom

For years, I had a dream.

Every time I walked past a particular designer store, I would pause and admire the window display. The dresses were stunning, elegant and timeless, but I never stepped inside. I told myself, *One day ... maybe when I have a special occasion, I'll buy one.*

Fast forward to this year and, suddenly, I had multiple special occasions. We had been lucky enough to be invited to several weddings, and I wanted to look and feel amazing at each one. That's when it hit me: *Maybe this is the time to finally buy that dress so I can wear the same dress to all the weddings.*

But there was one problem: This wasn't just any dress, it was a $700 dress.

Now, spending $700 on a dress isn't something I would normally do. My usual approach is to stick to more affordable outfits, maybe $100 or $200 max for something special. But this wasn't just any purchase, it was something I had wanted for years, something I knew I'd wear to every wedding, and something that made me feel incredible. And that's when my budgeting mindset kicked in.

Instead of impulsively swiping my card and dealing with the guilt later, I made a plan. I looked at my budget and decided that if I wanted this dress, I'd adjust a few things.

- I reduced my clothing budget for a few months: No new outfits, no casual shopping.
- I cut back on eating out: Instead of two or three restaurant meals a week, I opted for just one, and sometimes, instead of dinner out, I just grabbed a coffee, gelato or bubble tea, which was way cheaper but still fun.
- I made small swaps in my spending: Pausing non-essential purchases so I could reallocate that money toward the dress.

A few months later, I walked into that store and bought the dress — without guilt, without stress and knowing that my finances were still completely under control. And let me tell you, it felt so good.

What I've realised is: budgeting isn't about restriction, it's about freedom.

It's not about saying 'no' to things you love, it's about intentionally choosing where your money goes so you can say *'hell yes!'* to the things that truly matter to you.

And that's exactly what this chapter is about.

What's coming up next...

In this chapter, we're flipping the script on budgeting. Forget the boring spreadsheets and restrictive rules, this is about creating a budget that feels empowering, flexible and fun. You'll learn:

- the 3Fs of budgeting, and how to balance your money between foundation (essentials), fun (enjoying life) and freedom (investing in your future)
- why budgeting = freedom and how having a plan helps you spend guilt-free on what matters most
- to find your perfect balance by discovering a budgeting style that fits your life, not just some one-size-fits-all rule
- money tips for couples so you can manage finances with your partner without awkward convos or arguments
- budgeting hacks (like the 50/30/20 rule and pay yourself first) to keep your money on track — effortlessly.

The 3Fs of budgeting: Foundation, fun and freedom

One of the biggest misconceptions about budgeting is that it's all about restriction — no more $5 coffees, and basically the opposite of everything fun. But that couldn't be further from the truth. A great budget isn't about saying 'no', it's about saying 'yes' to the things that light you up. And the best way to do that is what I like to call the 3Fs of budgeting — let me explain.

This simple approach helps you balance your spending so you can enjoy life today while also setting yourself up for the future.

Foundation: Covering your essentials

Your *foundation* is the base of your financial house. It's the non-negotiable stuff, the things you need to live a stable life and the bare minimum that keeps your life running smoothly.

What's included?

- housing (rent or mortgage)
- utilities (electricity, water, internet)
- groceries
- transport
- insurance
- healthcare

This category usually takes up the biggest portion of your budget. A popular rule of thumb is to have it take up no more than 50 per cent of your income, but everyone's numbers will be different depending on their lifestyle, where they live and their personal financial goals.

Why is this important?

If your foundation isn't solid, if you're constantly struggling to cover rent or pay bills, then no amount of fun spending or investing will make you feel financially secure. Prioritising this category gives you peace of mind, knowing that your foundational needs are taken care of.

Fun: The things that make life exciting

Now, let's talk about the stuff that makes life *fun!* This category is all about spending on things that make you happy (remember our fun money from Chapter 1?), because what's the point of money if you don't get to enjoy it?

What's included?

- eating out
- coffee and snacks
- subscriptions (Netflix, Spotify, Disney+)

- clothes
- beauty
- hobbies and activities
- entertainment (movies, concerts, theme parks)
- travel

A common budgeting principle suggests 30 per cent of your income should go toward this category, but this will vary for everyone and even depend on the period of your life and your goals. The key is to spend on what makes you truly happy, not just mindless spending that doesn't add value to your life.

Why is this important?

If you only focus on saving and investing but never enjoy your money, life can start to feel dull and restrictive. I've been there. I once went through a phase of extreme saving, and even though I was doing 'the right thing' financially, I felt like I wasn't truly living. Having fun with your money is just as important as growing it.

Freedom: Investing in your future

The *freedom* category is what sets you up for long-term wealth and security. It's the money that your *future self* will thank you for. When you put money into this category, you're literally buying your future freedom — the ability to work less, retire early or have the financial flexibility to do whatever you want.

What's included?

- investing in shares, ETFs and index funds (see Chapter 8 for more on this)
- contributing to superannuation or retirement accounts
- investing in property or rental income (Chapter 9 covers this later)
- starting a business or side hustle
- building an emergency fund

A loose guideline is to allocate at least 20 per cent of your income to this category, but if you're aiming for financial independence, you might choose to invest even more.

Why is this important?

If you don't prioritise your future, one day you might wake up and realise you have no safety net, no investments and no way to step away from work if you want to. A strong freedom category ensures that you're not just living for today, but building a better tomorrow.

Finding the right balance for you

Now that you know the 3Fs (foundation, fun and freedom), how do you strike the right balance?

For many people, the 50/30/20 rule works well:

- 50 per cent on foundation (covering your needs)
- 30 per cent on fun (enjoy life now)
- 20 per cent on freedom (enjoy life later).

But here's the thing—there's no one-size-fits-all budget. Your percentages will depend on your income, lifestyle and financial priorities. For example:

- If you love travelling, you might allocate less to eating out and more to experiences.
- If you want to retire early, you might put more toward freedom and less toward fun.
- If you live in an expensive city, your foundation percentage might be higher.

The key is finding a balance that works for you — one that allows you to enjoy your money without guilt while still setting yourself up for long-term success.

Why you need to find the right balance in all three categories

Some people focus only on one or two of these categories, but here's why you need all three:

- If you have *foundation* + *fun*, but no freedom → You might be comfortable now, but you're not building for the future. In the future, you may find yourself in financial stress because you never invested.
- If you have *foundation* + *freedom*, but no fun → You're doing all the 'right' things, but life might feel restrictive. You might get burned out and feel like you're never enjoying your money or life.
- If you have *fun* + *freedom*, but no foundation → You might be living your best life and investing for the future, but if your essential needs aren't covered, financial instability will catch up with you.

The goal is *balance*.

Imagine this: You're sitting at a cafe, sipping your iced strawberry matcha (if you know, you know). You're enjoying every sip *guilt-free* because you know your budget is in perfect harmony: your foundation is strong, your fun money spending is intentional and your freedom investments are working for future you. That's the power of the 3Fs.

Money isn't about restriction, it's about designing a life you love — today, tomorrow and for the future. And with the Foundation, Fun and Freedom Formula, you'll be able to do exactly that.

Budgeting is making a plan for your money

A lot of people think budgeting is about cutting back and missing out. But, in reality, budgeting is about spending guilt-free because you've already taken care of your needs, your future investments and the things that bring you joy.

Here's the thing, your money is going to be spent, whether you plan it or not. The question is, are you happy with where it's going? When you create a budget, you're giving yourself the power to choose where your money goes, instead of wondering later where it all disappeared to.

Let's think about it like this: imagine going to the grocery store, but instead of bringing a shopping list, you decide to just 'wing it'. You wander the aisles, grabbing whatever looks good, and then suddenly you check the time and realise that two hours have just slipped by! Then you get home and realise you forgot the peanut butter — but somehow, you picked up an extra can of tomatoes, even though you already have three cans in the pantry. That's what happens when you wing it. Bringing a shopping list helps you ensure that you get exactly what you need while avoiding impulse purchases and wasted time.

Without a budget, your money has a way of slipping through your fingers. You might feel like you earn a decent income, yet somehow, there's nothing left at the end of the month, and you feel like you haven't even enjoyed anything you spent money on either! That's because, without a budget, money will always find somewhere to go — whether it's towards things that truly matter to you or not.

But when you budget intentionally, you take control. You get to tell your money where to go before it disappears. You can allocate money to help you fund your goals, your dreams and the life you actually want. And the best part is, you don't have to give up the fun stuff — you just plan for it. And that's the real secret to guilt-free spending.

How to create your budget

A good budget isn't just about the numbers, it's about what you want your money to do for you. It's how you make room for the things that matter while still covering your essentials and future goals.

In Chapter 5 I talked about the monthly ritual where Pablo and I look at where our money is going. We treat the exercise like detective work and I gave you some steps so you could also look at where your money is going and put that spending into categories. Now we can take that one step further and create a budget based on both your current spending and how you want to spend in the future.

This step is all about being intentional: putting in all your income sources, estimating your expected earnings and listing out all your expenses. Then, you can adjust based on your financial priorities. Table 6.1 shows an example of a budget breakdown.

Table 6.1: Example budget breakdown

Income			Expenses		
Source	*Frequency*	*Amount*	*Category*	*Frequency*	*Amount*
Salary	Monthly	$5000	Housing (rent or mortgage)	Monthly	$1700
Side hustle	Monthly	$300	Utilities	Monthly	$100
Total		$5300	Groceries	Monthly	$500
Savings			Eating out	Monthly	$200
Source	*Frequency*	*Amount*	Gym	Monthly	$250
Holiday	Monthly	$250	Gifts	Monthly	$100
Total		$250	Home (furniture and other items)	Monthly	$100
Investments			Health	Monthly	$100
Source	*Frequency*	*Amount*	Beauty	Monthly	$200
Shares	Monthly	$1000	Donations	Monthly	$100
Total		$1000	Clothes	Monthly	$200
			Car	Monthly	$100
			Insurance	Monthly	$100
			Entertainment	Monthly	$200
			Transport	Monthly	$100
			Total		$4050

Make sure you have a balance in your budget

The beauty of budgeting is you get to decide how you'd like to shift things around; for example, maybe you cut back on entertainment so you can save more for a dream holiday. The goal isn't to deprive yourself, it's to spend intentionally on what truly matters to you.

Automate and track your spending

The easiest way to stay on track is to automate your budget:

- Pay yourself first: Automatically transfer money to savings and investments as soon as you get paid.
- Use a budgeting tool: Tools like Billroo help you track spending effortlessly.
- Check in monthly: Review your budget, make adjustments and keep tweaking until it fits your lifestyle.

Budgeting isn't about sacrifice, it's about freedom. It's how you spend intentionally, without guilt, and make sure every dollar is working for you.

Budgeting methods

Here are a few budgeting methods to try.

The 50/30/20 budget: The classic, no-stress approach

On page 102 we talked about the 50/30/20 rule, which is a great place to start in setting up your budget because it's a simple framework that still gives you flexibility.

With the 50/30/20 rule, 50 per cent of your income goes to needs (housing, groceries, transport, bills), 30 per cent goes to wants (fun money: dining out, travel, shopping) and 20 per cent goes into your savings and investments (building wealth and securing your future).

The pay yourself first method (my personal favourite)

This is my go-to budgeting strategy because it flips the traditional spending mindset on its head. Instead of spending all your money first and saving whatever is left (if anything), you pay yourself first, meaning you put aside money for savings and investments before spending a single dollar on anything else.

How it works

1. Decide how much to save or invest (I personally aim for 20 to 30 per cent of my income).
2. Cover your essential expenses (rent/mortgage, groceries, bills, transport — anything that keeps life running smoothly).
3. Spend guilt-free on your wants (whatever is left is fun money and yours to enjoy without stressing over whether you've saved enough).

Warren Buffett, one of the richest people in the world, swears by this method: 'Do not save what is left after spending, but spend what is left after saving.'

Honestly, this method changed everything for me. I used to spend my paycheque first, and whatever was left at the end of the month (if anything) would go into savings. But now? My future self is always taken care of first, and I never feel guilty about spending the rest on things I love.

The multiple bank account method

This is a game-changer if you love organisation and automation. The idea is simple: You create separate bank accounts (or 'buckets') for different spending categories, and your paycheque is automatically divided among them.

How it works
- Account 1: Bills and essentials: This covers rent/mortgage, groceries, utilities — everything you need to survive.
- Account 2: Dining out, shopping, subscriptions, entertainment — fun money!
- Account 3: Savings and investments: Emergency fund, shares, retirement — money for future you.
- Account 4: Travel or big goals: If you love travelling, this is a great way to save for big adventures without dipping into your other funds.

The best part? It's automated. Once you set up direct deposits into these accounts, you don't even have to think about it — it just happens.

This method works amazingly well if you find yourself constantly transferring money back and forth or wondering where your paycheque disappeared to.

Zero-based budgeting: Every dollar has a job

If you're someone who loves detailed planning, this might be the method for you. Zero-based budgeting means that every single dollar of your income is assigned a job, whether it's for bills, savings, investing or fun. At the end of the month, your income minus expenses equals zero.

How it works
1. Write down your total monthly income.
2. List out all your expenses (including savings and investments).
3. Assign a purpose to every dollar so that your income minus expenses = $0.

This method forces you to be intentional with your money and helps prevent mindless spending. If you've ever found yourself thinking, *Where did all my money go?* at the end of the month, zero-based budgeting can help you track exactly where every dollar is going.

Which budgeting method is right for you?

Budgeting is not a one-size-fits-all situation. The best method is the one that:

- feels natural to you
- helps you stay consistent
- allows you to spend guilt-free while still saving for the future.

At the end of the day, a budget is just a plan for how you want to use your money. It should never feel restrictive; it should feel empowering.

So, experiment, try out different budgeting methods, and adapt them to fit your life. Because the best budget is the one that actually works for you.

Managing money as a couple

When Pablo and I first moved in together, we were so excited, but there was one thing we hadn't really thought about: how to split our expenses.

Neither of us had ever lived with a partner before, so we just went with what seemed like the most obvious approach: splitting everything 50/50. It made sense at first, after all, that's what you'd do with a roommate, right? We divided up rent, groceries and bills evenly, and for the first couple of months, it *kind of* worked.

But there was one big problem: I was still a student, only working part-time, while Pablo had a full-time job. I was making half of what he was earning, but I was still trying to cover the same expenses. By the end of each month, I barely had anything left for myself. While Pablo could still afford to go out, buy new clothes or even just save some money, I was struggling to keep up.

At first, I didn't want to say anything. I felt like I *should* be able to contribute equally. But after a few months of constantly stressing about money, I finally told Pablo that the 50/50 split just wasn't working for me. He completely understood, and that's when we decided to split our expenses based on our incomes instead.

Switching to a proportional split made a *huge* difference. Instead of both of us paying the same amount, we each contributed a percentage of our income. Since Pablo was earning more, he covered a larger portion of our shared expenses, and I contributed what I could afford. This way, neither of us felt financially drained, and we both had room to breathe.

It worked really well for a while, but then something changed — I started earning more. I got a full-time job and, suddenly, we were making similar amounts. Since our incomes were now more equal, it made sense to go back to splitting everything 50/50.

But then, there was another change and I started earning more than Pablo. This time, instead of changing how we split expenses, we decided on a different approach. We still kept things 50/50, but since I had extra income, I contributed more to our home deposit and our investments. That way, we could buy our first home faster, without putting financial pressure on Pablo to match my contributions.

It wasn't just about covering expenses anymore: We were working toward shared financial goals, and we found a way to balance things in a way that felt fair.

Now, we're in a completely different stage of our lives. We both quit our jobs to run our business together, so we pay ourselves exactly the same amount. We do mostly have shared finances now. We invest all of our money together and, for the most part, don't consider things as 'his' or 'mine' anymore, but 'ours', but, we still like to keep our separate accounts for a bit of independence.

What we've learned about managing money as a couple

Looking back, I love how our approach to money has evolved with our relationship. In the beginning, we thought we had to stick to one way of splitting expenses forever. But the reality is, your financial system should change as your life changes.

When I was a student, splitting 50/50 was stressful and unrealistic, but later, when we were earning similar amounts, it felt totally fair. And when I started earning more than Pablo, I could help us reach our financial goals without making Pablo feel like he had to contribute the same amount.

The thing about managing money in a relationship is there's no right or wrong way to do it. The best approach is the one that feels fair to both of you and allows you to support each other while still having financial independence.

We're going to break down different ways you and your partner can split expenses so you can find what works for you. Whether you're in a brand-new relationship or have been together for years, managing money as a couple is always a learning experience. And just like Pablo and me, you might find that your approach changes over time. It's important to keep talking about it and adjusting the way you manage your finances as your situations may change over time.

How to manage finances as a couple (without fighting over money)

Talking about money in a relationship can feel awkward at first, but let's be real, it's one of the biggest factors in long-term happiness. Whether you're moving in together for the first time or have been sharing finances for years, figuring out how to manage finances in a way that feels fair is so important.

If you're trying to figure out the best way to manage finances with your partner, here are some of the most common ways couples do it, along with the pros, cons and how to make each one work for *you*.

The 50/50 split

This is where most couples start. With the 50/50 split, everything is split evenly down the middle: rent, groceries, bills etc.

Best for: Couples with similar incomes and expenses.

How it works: You both contribute the same amount to shared expenses, regardless of income differences.

Example: Your total shared expenses are $3000 per month, so each person contributes $1500.

Pros:

- Super simple; no calculations needed.
- Encourages financial independence.
- Works well when both partners earn similar incomes.

Cons:

- Can feel unfair if one person earns significantly more.
- Might financially strain the lower-earning partner.

Who this is great for: If you and your partner earn similar salaries, this method keeps things clean, simple and fair. If one of you earns way more, it can quickly feel like one person is struggling while the other has extra spending money.

The proportional split

This method is for couples who earn different amounts but want to contribute in a way that feels proportionally fair.

Best for: Couples with big income differences.

How it works: Each person contributes a percentage of their income instead of splitting everything 50/50.

Example: Partner A earns $6000/month and Partner B earns $4000/month, which makes their total income $10 000. Since Partner A earns 60 per cent of the total income, they cover 60 per cent of expenses, while Partner B covers 40 per cent.

If shared expenses are $3000 per month, that means Partner A pays $1800 and Partner B pays $1200.

Pros:
- Feels fairer than a strict 50/50 split.
- Prevents financial strain on the lower-earning partner.

Cons:
- The higher-earning partner might feel like they're paying more than their fair share.
- It can be a little tricky to calculate.

Who this is great for: If one of you earns significantly more, this method ensures that you're both contributing fairly without leaving one person feeling broke while the other lives comfortably.

The 'you cover this, I cover that' method

Some couples prefer to skip the math and just divide expenses by category. Instead of splitting everything equally or proportionately, each person takes responsibility for certain bills.

Best for: Couples who don't want to constantly transfer money back and forth.

How it works: One partner pays for rent and utilities, while the other covers groceries, subscriptions and eating out.

Example: Partner A covers rent and utilities; Partner B covers groceries, dining out and transport.

Pros:

- Reduces constant calculations and money transfers.
- Each partner knows what they're responsible for.

Cons:

- Can feel uneven if expenses aren't distributed fairly.
- Might lead to resentment if one partner feels like they're paying more.

Who this is great for: If you and your partner prefer a clear division of financial responsibilities, this method can keep things really simple. Just make sure one person isn't covering more than the other.

The pooled approach

This method is all about pooling your money into a joint account and paying for everything from there.

Best for: Couples who want a structured system.

How it works: Each partner contributes a set amount into a joint account, which covers all shared expenses.

Example: You both agree to contribute $2000 per month to the joint account, and rent, groceries and bills are paid directly from this account.

Pros:

- Automates financial management.
- Promotes teamwork and transparency.
- No need to track who owes what.

Cons:

- Requires trust and communication.
- Can feel restrictive if one partner prefers separate finances.

Who this is great for: If you're married or in a long-term partnership, this can make managing money way easier. Just make sure you set clear expectations about personal spending.

Variation: You can combine this method with proportional contributions, meaning each partner deposits a percentage of their income into the joint account while also maintaining separate savings.

The hybrid approach

Some couples like a little independence but also want a shared system for big expenses.

Best for: Couples who want both independence and teamwork.

How it works: Each partner keeps a personal account for individual spending. Shared expenses are split 50/50 or proportionally. A joint account is used for savings, travel or big purchases.

Example: You split rent and groceries proportionally, but keep personal spending money for fun purchases. You save for holidays together in a shared account.

Pros:

- Flexible: each partner maintains financial independence.
- Works well for couples with different spending habits.

Cons:

- Requires regular money check-ins to stay on the same page.
- Might still involve some expense tracking.

Who this is great for: If you and your partner like having some financial independence but still want to plan together, this method gives you the best of both worlds.

Fully shared finances

This is the ultimate joint approach — everything is merged. There's no 'my money' or 'your money', it's *'our'* money.

Best for: Married couples or long-term partners with fully shared financial goals.

How it works: All income and savings go into one shared account, and both partners spend from the same pool of money, regardless of individual earnings.

Example: You and your partner each deposit your salaries into a single joint account, and all bills, rent, groceries and investments are paid from this account. Instead of tracking who owes what, you operate as one financial unit.

Pros:

- Super simple: no splitting, no tracking.
- Promotes full financial transparency.
- Makes long-term planning easier (for buying a house, retiring, etc.).

Cons:

- Can feel restrictive if one partner prefers financial independence.
- Risky if the relationship ends (especially without agreements in place).

Who this is great for: If you and your partner are completely aligned on financial goals and spending habits, this method eliminates a lot of hassle. But if one of you prefers having personal spending money, this can feel a bit too merged.

Variation: Some couples keep a joint account for big expenses (rent, investments, etc.) while maintaining separate accounts for personal spending.

Your turn: Which method is right for you?

As a couple, you may want to explore options that align with the following situations. If you:

- earn similar amounts, try a 50/50 split
- earn different amounts, consider a proportional split
- prefer separate finances, try the 'you cover this, I cover that' method
- want ease and automation, look into a pooled approach
- want flexibility, explore a hybrid approach
- want full financial unity, give fully shared finances a go.

As I've said, there is no one-size-fits-all approach. You may think you are an all-in, fully shared couple, only to find you crave some financial separation. Whatever method you choose, schedule regular money check-ins to make sure it's working for both of you. Finances change over time, and your system should evolve with you.

At the end of the day, managing money as a couple isn't just about paying bills, it's about building a life together that supports both your shared and personal goals.

Key takeaways

- Budgeting = freedom: It's not about restriction, it's about creating a plan that lets you spend guilt-free on what matters most.
- The 3Fs of budgeting: Balance your money between foundation (essentials), fun (enjoyment) and freedom (future goals) to live well now and later.
- Personalise your budget: There's no one-size-fits-all. Find a system that works for *you*, whether it's the 50/30/20 rule, pay yourself first or a hybrid approach.
- Money and relationships: There's no 'right' way to split expenses, just what feels fair and works for both of you. Keep communication open as your life and relationship evolves.
- Automate for success: Set it, forget it and let automation do the heavy lifting so you can focus on living your life.

In a nutshell

Budgeting isn't about saying 'no', it's about saying 'yes' with intention. When you've got a plan, you're in control, and that means more freedom to enjoy life without the stress of wondering where your money went.

Now that you've got your budget sorted, it's time to take it to the next level. In the next chapter, we'll explore how to save money without sucking the fun out of life. Because saving doesn't have to be boring—it can actually be exciting, addictive and even... fun. Yep, I said it. Let's go!

Chapter 7
SAVE without sucking the fun from life

When Pablo and I were saving for our first home, a lot of people assumed we were living like hermits: eating plain rice, saying 'no' to every social event and generally just suffering through the process. There's this idea that saving money means sucking all the fun out of life.

What we realised was that, sometimes, saving money can be just as fun as spending it, and it was a game-changer for our finances.

Instead of seeing our budget as a restriction, we turned it into a challenge. Each month, we'd track each dollar we spent and, at the end of the month, we'd sit down and see who had spent the least. The winner got bragging rights, which (let's be real) was more valuable than any actual prize.

But the best part wasn't just the game itself—it was seeing our savings grow. Every month, our home deposit crept higher, and instead of feeling deprived, we felt as though we had accomplished something. It was like playing a real-life version of Monopoly, except instead of collecting tiny green houses on a board, we were stacking up real savings toward an actual home.

And while we cut back in some areas, like packing homemade lunches for work instead of eating out, and were mindful of how small expenses added up, we made sure to keep spending on the things that mattered most to us. For us, that was travel.

It took us four years to save a $100 000 deposit, but even during that time, we still managed to travel. We went to Europe (we booked our flights during off-peak season to save money). We also travelled to Bali, Malaysia, Thailand and Tokyo, but we did it in a smart way. We found travel deals, used airline points and booked accommodation that gave us the best value.

This was one of the biggest mindset shifts we had: you don't have to give up what you love to save money, you just have to be strategic about it.

By cutting back in areas we didn't care about and being mindful with our spending, we got to enjoy the best of both worlds. We could still experience life, travel the world and build our financial future — all at the same time.

Our mindset made saving *exciting*. It didn't feel like a sacrifice. Instead of focusing on what we *couldn't* do, we focused on finding smart ways to still do the things we loved while making progress on our goals.

Most people *think* saving is about sacrifice, but the key to building wealth isn't just about cutting back, it's about enjoying the process as much as you enjoy spending. When saving feels like a game, it becomes addictive in the best way.

If you can find a way to make saving just as exciting as spending, you can actually enjoy the process of saving, and that's how you win the long game. And that's what this chapter is all about.

> **What's coming up next...**
>
> This chapter flips the script on saving because it doesn't have to suck the fun out of life! You'll discover:
>
> - how to make saving addictive (in the best way) by turning it into a game
> - the power of meaningful goals that actually excite you to save
> - why small rewards matter — and how they can supercharge your motivation
> - the 'save some, spend some' rule to enjoy life while growing your savings
> - how to break big goals into bite-sized wins (and celebrate every milestone)
> - the magic of dual savings pools so you can live your best life now *and* later.
>
> Get ready to save smarter, have more fun and build wealth without feeling like you're missing out. Let's make saving exciting!

Why you need to set meaningful savings goals

It's easy to say, *I want to save more money,* but without a clear and meaningful reason behind it, saving just for the sake of saving feels boring and uninspiring.

If you don't feel excited about your financial goals, how likely are you to stick with them? Not very likely, that's for sure. That's why choosing goals that actually mean something to you is the key to making saving enjoyable and sustainable.

Take our home deposit goal as an example.

When Pablo and I decided to save for our first home, we set a very specific target for our deposit: $100 000. That number wasn't just some random figure. It represented something tangible, something we could envision: a home of our own, our own space to live in, a place we could build our future in.

Because we had such a clear goal, every dollar we saved felt exciting, not restrictive. Every time we saw our balance grow, it wasn't just 'money in the bank', it was a step closer to a place we could call home.

Had we just said, *we should probably save some money*, it wouldn't have been nearly as motivating. Without a strong reason behind the goal, the process of cutting back and budgeting would have felt like a chore rather than an adventure.

The science behind meaningful goals

It turns out, there's actual research to back this up.

A study examined the relationship between achievement goals and life satisfaction. Researchers found that people who set meaningful and personally significant goals reported higher levels of happiness and fulfilment.

Why? Because when your goals align with what you truly care about, working toward them feels like a joy, not an obligation.

So whether you're saving for a house, a dream holiday or financial security for your family, make sure your goals excite you. They should spark something inside you that makes you want to keep going — even when it gets tough.

Instead of setting generic goals like:

- ✗ I should save more money
- ✗ I need to build an emergency fund...

...try reframing them in a way that connects with your values and emotions:

- ✔ I want to save $5000 so I can take my parents on a dream holiday to thank them for everything they've done for me.
- ✔ I'm building an emergency fund of $20 000 so I never have to stress about money again and can have peace of mind.
- ✔ I'm saving $20 000 for my first home because I want to create a space that's truly mine.

If you connect your financial goals to something you genuinely care about, every dollar saved feels like progress toward something bigger, something that makes you happy.

So before you start your next savings goal, ask yourself:

- Why does this matter to me?
- What will this money allow me to do that brings me joy, freedom or peace of mind?

Because when your goals are exciting, saving money stops feeling like something you have to do, and starts feeling like something you want to do. And that's how you win the game.

The power of small rewards

Saving money can feel like a long, slow journey. When you're working toward a big goal, it's easy to lose motivation. That's why celebrating small wins along the way is so important.

One of the best things Pablo and I did when we were saving for our first home was build in small rewards to keep us motivated.

How we made saving exciting without blowing our budget

While we were saving for our house deposit, we kept a spreadsheet that tracked every dollar. Since we had separate finances, we'd log any extra money we received, such as tax returns or side hustles, and decide how much to contribute to our shared investment account (which we were using to grow our home deposit).

This became a little game for us. Every few weeks, we'd update the spreadsheet, and if we had any extra money, we'd decide how much to invest. Watching that number grow was incredibly satisfying — it felt like we were levelling up in a financial game.

But we didn't just save, we rewarded ourselves along the way.

Celebrating every milestone (with bubble tea and gelato)

Every time we hit a savings milestone, say, every $5000, we made sure to celebrate, but not in a way that would undo all our hard work. We kept it small, fun and guilt-free, such as:

- a bubble tea date
- pastries or gelato
- going out for a coffee at our favourite cafe
- trying a new activity (like an outdoor cinema or wakeboarding).

None of these things were expensive (most of them cost under $20), but they made the whole journey so much more enjoyable. Instead of feeling like we were depriving ourselves, we had these little milestones to look forward to.

The rewards didn't have to be extravagant, just meaningful.

The 'save some, spend some' rule

Another way we kept saving fun was by rewarding ourselves when we earned extra money.

I remember one time when I worked a side hustle event over the weekend. It was a long day and when I got home, I was exhausted. But then I got paid, and Pablo said something that stuck with me: 'How about you spend half of it on whatever you want, and save the other half?'

Honestly, if it had been just me, I probably would have saved the whole thing, but this mindset shift made so much sense. I had put in the extra effort to work that event, so why not enjoy some of the reward while still staying on track with our financial goals?

After that, I started applying the same rule to other windfalls: tax returns, bonuses, even cash back rewards. Spending a portion of that money guilt-free made saving feel a lot more sustainable, and it kept me motivated to keep going.

The science behind small rewards

A study by BioSpace found that individuals who received immediate, frequent rewards for completing small tasks showed increased interest and motivation.

Why does this work?

- Immediate rewards keep you engaged: If you only celebrate at the very end, you might lose steam before you get there. Small wins keep the journey exciting.
- Dopamine reinforcement: Our brains love instant gratification, so let's use it to our advantage and give ourselves a small treat to reinforce a good habit.
- Progress feels real: When you acknowledge how far you've come, you're more likely to keep going.

Breaking your goals into smaller pieces

When you think about saving $10000 or $20000, it sounds like a huge, impossible mountain to climb. But what if we broke it down into bite-sized steps?

Let's say your goal is to save $20000 in one year. That's a huge number. But when you break it down, it's $1667 per month or about $385 per week or just $55 per day. Suddenly, it feels much more manageable.

What about $10000 in one year? That's $833 per month, $192 per week or $27 per day. Again, totally doable if you find ways to trim expenses, earn a little extra or set up automatic transfers.

Even a smaller goal, like $5000 in a year is just $416 per month, $96 per week or $14 per day. That's the price of a couple of coffees and a snack.

And if you're starting small, say saving $1000 in a year, that's only $83 per month, $19 per week or just $3 per day. That's literally loose change.

See how powerful breaking it down is? Instead of feeling like you need to magically come up with thousands of dollars, you just need to focus on hitting your next small milestone.

Have a dual savings pool

A lot of people think that once you invest or save money, it's locked away forever, like some kind of financial black hole. But your money is yours, and you can access it whenever you need it. That's why I love the dual savings pool approach: one for now and one for later. It gives you flexibility, freedom and financial security all at the same time.

We're going to discuss dual savings pools in more detail in Chapter 11, where we explain how to take mini-retirements, but here's a little teaser for you. The idea is to set up two different savings pools that work for your short-, medium- and long-term plans.

Pool #1: Short- to medium-term savings and investments

This is money you can easily access when you need it, such as investments in stocks or ETFs, or a high-interest savings account. It's for things like travel, buying a home, upgrading your lifestyle or taking time off work if you need it.

Pool #2: Long-term savings and retirement funds

This is money you *won't* touch for decades. Think superannuation, retirement accounts or long-term investments that you plan to hold for 20+ years. It's the safety net that ensures future you is financially secure.

By intentionally separating your money into different savings pools, you can mentally separate how these two lots of money are working for you, and not feel as though dipping into your short- to medium-term savings is setting your long-term future back.

Your turn: Make saving a game

Saving doesn't feel restrictive when you create a meaningful goal and gamify your progress towards it. Follow these steps to set a meaningful savings goal and break it down into smaller steps.

Step 1: Define your goal

It's important to choose a goal that you're actually excited about; for example, a holiday to Japan, a home deposit, an emergency fund or something else meaningful.

My savings goal: _____

Target amount: $_____

Timeframe: _____ months

Step 2: Break it down

Breaking down your big goal into smaller pieces makes it so much less daunting; for example, a $5000 goal over 12 months means saving:

- $5000 ÷ 12 months = $417 per month
- $5000 ÷ 52 weeks = $96 per week
- $5000 ÷ 365 days = $14 per day

Step 3: Choose a savings challenge

You could also create a savings challenge for yourself so you can gamify it! Pick one (or more):

- No-spend challenge: Cut out one expense for a set period and transfer the savings.
- Round-up hack: Use an app or manually round up purchases and save the difference.
- Spending swap: Replace an expensive habit with a lower-cost alternative and save the difference (e.g., rather than buying a coffee out every day, challenge yourself to make one at home a few days a week).
- Milestone rewards: Set checkpoints (e.g., every $1000 saved) and allow yourself a small, planned reward.

Step 4: Track your progress

Use a simple table or app to track your savings and stay motivated.

Milestone	Target savings	Amount saved	Reward (if applicable)
Week 1	$100		
Week 4	$400		
Month 6	$2500		

Step 5: Celebrate your wins

It's so important to enjoy the journey and celebrate your wins along the way. Choose a meaningful, budget-friendly way to acknowledge progress that doesn't undo your hard work.

First milestone reward: _____

Key takeaways

- Saving doesn't have to suck: When you make it fun, it becomes addictive in the best way.
- Meaningful goals = motivated saving: The more your goals excite you, the easier it is to stay on track.
- Celebrate small wins: Little rewards keep you motivated without derailing your progress.
- Break big goals into bite-sized chunks: Focusing on daily, weekly or monthly targets makes saving feel achievable.
- The 'save some, spend some' rule rocks: Enjoying a portion of unexpected money keeps saving sustainable.
- Dual savings pools = freedom: One for now, one for later so you can enjoy life and build wealth at the same time.

In a nutshell

Saving is the foundation of financial freedom, but it's only part of the story. Once you've mastered the art of saving without sacrificing the things you love, the next step is to make your money work *for* you.

In the next chapter, we'll break down the basics of investing, show you how to grow your wealth with ease, and prove that you don't need to be a finance expert to build a powerful portfolio. Get ready to unlock the next level of your money game.

Chapter 8
INVEST with confidence

When Pablo and I first started investing, we were *all in*. We started off simply using a robo-adviser to invest in a diversified portfolio without too much effort. Then, we thought, we may as well lower the fees and pick our own exchange traded funds (ETFs) and investments. So that's what we did.

That's when, we got a little... overconfident.

We thought, *Surely, we can do better than this. ETFs and diversified portfolios just track the market, but why not beat the market?*

So, we dove headfirst into researching individual stocks, and not just casually — we went full detective mode.

Imagine two people hunched over their laptops, spreadsheets open, multiple browser tabs filled with financial reports, CEO interviews, balance sheets, earnings calls and deep dives into PE (price-to-earnings) ratios, market trends and competitive advantages. At one point, we even found ourselves reading Warren Buffett's old shareholder letters.

Hours turned into days. Days turned into weeks.

And then... nothing.

We didn't invest in *anything*.

We got so caught up in finding the perfect strategy, the perfect stock and the perfect timing that we ended up doing what most over-researchers do — we did absolutely nothing.

By the time we finally convinced ourselves that a stock was worth buying, we'd either missed the best buying opportunity or convinced ourselves it wasn't the right price yet, so we'd wait... and wait... and wait...

And then, months later, we'd look back and see that the stock we were waiting for had doubled in price while we were just sitting on the sidelines with a pile of cash.

That's when we realised something big: *overcomplicating investing is the fastest way to not invest at all.*

The biggest investing mistake is not investing at all...

This was a huge lesson for us: If you make investing hard, you just won't do it, and by not investing, you're actually *losing* money.

A study by Dalbar Inc. looked at investor behaviour over 30 years, and found that the average investor underperformed in the market by significant margins — not because they were bad at picking stocks, but because they tried to time the market and overcomplicated everything.

Instead of just keeping it simple and investing consistently, they hesitated, got scared, jumped in and out of the market, and missed out on long-term gains.

What we learned about keeping it simple

What we eventually learned (after all that unnecessary stress) is that the easiest investing strategy is often the best one.

- Automate it: Set up automatic investments so you don't have to think about it.
- Stick to diversified investments: ETFs, for example, can give you solid returns without all the guesswork.
- Invest consistently: Instead of trying to time the market, invest regularly (a strategy called dollar-cost averaging).

That's why, in this chapter, we're going to talk about how to make investing as effortless as possible so you don't fall into the trap of overthinking and missing out.

Time in the market beats timing the market—and the sooner you start, the better.

> ### What's coming up next...
>
> This chapter breaks down the myths, fears and confusion around investing so you can start growing your wealth with confidence. Together, we'll explore:
>
> - why keeping it simple beats trying to 'outsmart' the market (even Warren Buffett agrees)
> - the ultimate showdown: saving vs investing and when to do them
> - the two must-dos before you invest: build an emergency fund and tackle high-interest debt

(continued)

> - how to start investing step by step — no finance degree required
> - the magic of compound interest and why your first $100k is the hardest (but it gets easier!)
> - how to manage your emotions during market crashes so you don't sabotage your own success.
>
> By the end of this chapter, you'll see that investing isn't about luck, perfect timing or picking the next big stock — it's about consistency, simplicity and letting time do the heavy lifting. Let's get your money working for you.

Should you save or invest?

Okay, so you've got $1000 a month to put somewhere. Should you save it in a high-interest bank account or should you invest it?

Let's run the numbers and find out.

Option 1: Saving $1000 per month in a 5 per cent high-interest bank account

Let's say you diligently put $1000 per month into a high-interest savings account that offers 5 per cent per year for 40 years.

Total saved: $1000 per month for 40 years

Final amount after 40 years: ~$1.53 million

Not bad, right? You saved consistently, earned some interest and ended up a millionaire.

But what if you invested instead?

Option 2: Investing $1000 per month in the stock market (8 per cent return)

Now, let's say instead of just saving, you put that same $1000 per month into an ETF that tracks the stock market, returning an average 8 per cent per year.

Final amount after 40 years: ~$3.49 million

That's over $1.9 million *more* than just saving!

That's the magic of compound interest in action. A 3 per cent difference in returns (5 vs 8 per cent) may not seem like much at first, but over 40 years, it creates an enormous gap.

Why investing wins over the long term

Here's the thing: saving money is great for short-term goals, but investing for the long term is where the real magic happens!

Your money earns returns → Your returns earn more returns → Your wealth snowballs.

This is why the rich keep getting richer, because they let compound interest do the heavy lifting instead of just relying on their paycheque.

But wait... saving is important too!

This doesn't mean you should never save money (and if you've already read Chapter 7, you are well on your way). Saving is essential for:

- emergency funds (three to six months of expenses)
- short-term goals (big purchases within the next five years)
- a buffer for unexpected life events.

High-interest savings accounts are safe and predictable, which makes them perfect for things you'll need soon, but if you want serious wealth over the long term?

Investing is the way to go.

Final verdict: Save for short-term vs invest for the long-term

- 0 to 5 years? → use a high-interest savings account
- 5+ years? → invest in assets like stocks, property etc.

Before you start investing: Get these things sorted first

I know, I know — you're probably super pumped to start investing, and trust me, I get it! Watching your money grow while you do literally nothing is — *chef's kiss* — amazing. But before we dive into the world of ETFs and index funds, there are two major things you need to check off first.

Skipping these steps is like going skydiving without checking if your parachute is working: it might be fine, but if things go south, you'll wish you were prepared.

Step 1: Build your emergency fund

Life doesn't always go to plan. Your car breaks down, your pet suddenly needs surgery or, *plot twist,* your boss decides your job is 'no longer required'. If all your money is locked up in investments, you might be forced to sell them at a bad time, such as when the market is down. And trust me, selling investments in a downturn *hurts*.

That's why you need an emergency fund — your financial safety net for when life throws curveballs.

What's an emergency fund?

- A stash of three to six months of living expenses saved in cash.
- It's there for real emergencies (think job loss, medical expenses or surprise bills).

Where should you keep it?
- A high-interest savings account so your money earns a little extra while it sits.
- An offset account (if you have a mortgage), which can help reduce the interest you pay on your home loan.

How to build it (even if you're starting from $0)
- Start small: If saving three to six months' worth of expenses feels impossible, aim for $1000.
- Automate it: Set up a direct debit to a separate savings account so you don't even think about it.
- Boost it over time: Once you hit $1000, work towards one month's expenses, then two, and so on.

Hot tip: Don't confuse an emergency fund with a 'treat yourself' fund. A cheap flight to Bali is *not* an emergency, but a last-minute root canal is.

Step 2: Pay off high-interest debt

Before investing, you also want to tackle bad debt (aka debt that's eating up your money faster than you can make it).

What counts as high-interest debt?
- Credit card debt (15 to 20 per cent interest)
- Personal loans (12 to 20 per cent)
- Buy now, pay later schemes (yep, those sneaky fees add up!)

Why pay this off before investing?

Paying off debt gives you a guaranteed return. Let's say you're paying 18 per cent interest on a credit card. If you pay off that debt, it's like getting an instant 18 per cent return on your money — risk-free!

There's almost no investment in the world that can promise you 18 per cent returns *guaranteed*. Even if the stock market averages 8 to 10 per cent a year, that's still *way* lower than what you're losing to high-interest debt.

How to get out of bad debt faster

Focus on anything above 8 per cent interest first: this is where the real damage happens.

Use the avalanche method: Pay off the highest-interest debt first while making minimum payments on the rest.

Try the snowball method: Pay off the smallest debt first while making minimum payments on the rest. Once it's cleared, roll that payment over to the next smallest debt. The great thing about this method is it builds your confidence and momentum, just like a snowball rolling down a hill!

Step 3: Automate payments so you don't forget

Once your high-interest debt is gone, you can relax about lower-interest debt (like mortgages or student loans). These aren't as urgent to pay down unless you personally want to.

You're ready to invest

Once you've got a solid emergency fund in place and cleared your high-interest debt, you're ready to start investing.

At this point, you can start putting your money to work in ETFs, or whatever investment strategy excites you. And the best part is, because you've handled your financial foundation first, you can invest stress-free knowing you won't have to panic-sell at the worst time.

Why it's important to keep it simple

Everyone loves the idea of beating the market: picking that one stock that skyrockets, making a fortune and retiring to a beach house before 40. It sounds like the dream, right?

But, let's get real. Trying to outsmart the market is like trying to outswim a shark—it's possible in theory, but in reality, you're probably gonna lose. And the research backs this up.

I'm going to share a story that shows that the best strategy isn't about being the smartest, fastest or most aggressive investor, it's about keeping it simple.

Warren Buffett's million-dollar Wall Street bet

Imagine this. You're at a fancy restaurant, sipping on a cocktail, and some hedge fund managers (let's call them Chad, Brad and Greg) start bragging about their stock-picking skills.

They're throwing around big words like *arbitrage*, *derivatives* and *market inefficiencies*, flexing about how they beat the market every year.

Enter American billionaire and renowned investor Warren Buffett.

Buffett, in his usual chill, grandpa-like wisdom, listens to their finance bro monologue and then bets them a million dollars that they're all full of it.

His challenge was simple:

- He picks one simple, low-cost S&P 500 index fund, which just tracks the top 500 US companies and does nothing fancy.
- Chad, Brad and Greg get to pick a bunch of hedge funds (aka elite, professionally managed funds that charge high fees but promise mind-blowing returns).

Then they would see who wins after ten years.

Who do you think won?

The hedge funds (managed by Wall Street's 'best and brightest') returned just 2.2 per cent per year, barely outpacing inflation.

Buffett's boring index fund performed at 7.1 per cent per year — more than triple the hedge funds' returns.

While the hedge funds were busy making complicated trades, adjusting their portfolios and charging their investors high fees, Buffett just sat back, did nothing and still won.

Wall Street's smartest investors (people with billion-dollar research teams) got absolutely wrecked by a simple low-cost index fund that costs almost nothing to own.

So next time you try to do a Queenie and Pablo from page 131 and go full detective mode, take a step back and think about it. If hedge fund managers can't consistently beat the market, how can the average person?

Remember: you don't need to be a finance genius to invest successfully, you just need to keep it simple. Index funds and ETFs win because they don't try to be smart, they just ride the market's long-term growth.

Passive investments vs active investments

If you still need convincing, here's another interesting study that looked at how well actively managed investment funds (funds where professionals try to pick winning stocks) performed against passive index funds (which just follow the market).

You might think that the finance people in fancy suits — with their degrees and multiple computer screens with stock graphs — would have an edge when it comes to investing, but multiple studies show that, over time, most of them fail to beat the market.

A study by S&P Dow Jones Indices tracked how well actively managed investment funds perform against simple, low-cost index funds (like the S&P 500). The results were pretty surprising:

- Over a ten-year period, 79.6 per cent of actively managed US equity funds lost to the S&P Composite 1500 Index.
- Over 15 years, the number jumped even higher: 90 per cent of actively managed funds failed to beat the market.
- And here's the kicker: even the few funds that do win in one year often lose in the next.

But wait — maybe this is just a US thing? Nope. Morningstar's Active-Passive Barometer reached the same conclusion:

- Over a ten-year period, most active funds underperformed passive funds across nearly every investment category.
- The more expensive the fund, the worse it performed.
- The *cheaper* an active fund was, the more it resembled a *passive* fund.

So the lesson is simple: Most active funds don't out perform the market.

Why does this happen?

So why do actively managed funds typically lose to index funds?

The stock market is unpredictable

Even the best investors don't have a crystal ball. Market movements are influenced by global events, economic shifts and, let's be honest, sometimes just pure chaos *(looking at you, meme stocks)*.

High fees can eat into gains

Active funds charge management fees, trading fees and performance fees, which can eat into your returns.

We're only human

Fund managers are human, and humans make emotional decisions. They, too, can panic-sell at the wrong time and chase hot stocks.

What it means for us

So if we want to be successful investors, we need to:

- Stick to a simple strategy.
- Ignore short-term market noise: investing is a long game.

The market will go up and down in the short term, but it trends upwards over time, so just let it do its thing.

And remember: If most professionals can't beat the market, why waste your time trying? That's why it's recommended to stick with index funds or ETFs, and watch your money grow.

CHESS-sponsored brokers

CHESS stands for Clearing House Electronic Subregister System — it's the Australian Stock Exchange's (ASX) way of recording share ownership. When you buy shares with a CHESS-sponsored broker, you receive a unique holder identification number (HIN) directly from the ASX, meaning you legally own the shares in your name.

It's comparable to having your name on the deed to a house versus having someone else hold the deed for you. If an investing app were to disappear tomorrow, your shares would still be yours because they're registered directly in your name with the ASX.

Some platforms use a custodian model where the company technically owns the shares on your behalf. While often cheaper to operate, this adds a layer of risk if the custodian isn't very reputable. So it's important to look into who the custodian is — usually this will be an external company.

It's also important to note that CHESS sponsorship is only for Australian shares. In the US and other global markets, there is no CHESS sponsorship. Shares you buy outside of the ASX will be held with a custodian.

How to start investing step by step

Investing might sound fancy, but it's actually quite easy once you get the hang of it. Think of it like planting a money tree: water it, give it some time and watch it grow. Here's your step-by-step guide to start investing today, no stress required.

Step 1: Pick your investing app

Investing apps make it easy for anyone to start. If you have the skills to buy a pair of shoes on your phone, then you have the skills to make an investment — that's how easy it is these days. Just pick one with low fees (because why pay more?) and features like CHESS sponsorship (in Australia) if that's your vibe.

I've created table 8.1 (overleaf) for you to compare some popular options for investing apps.

Step 2: Open your account

It's like signing up for Netflix, but instead of endless binges, you get one step closer to financial freedom. The apps listed in table 8.1 are all great choices, but it also depends on what your vibe is. I personally use Pearler because of their low fees and great autoinvest features, and I love how it's designed for long-term investors but, honestly, I've tried many of these investing apps and they're all really good! The best part is that setting up an account is free, and you can always switch apps later if you find a better fit.

Table 8.1: Australian investing apps compared

App	Brokerage fees	Autoinvest?	CHESS sponsored?	Markets
CMC Markets	$0 fee to buy trades under $1000 in a single day $11 or 0.10% after	Yes	Yes	ASX, US international
CommSec	$5 up to and including $1000 $10 between $1000.01 and $3000 $19.95 between $3000.01 and $10000 $29.95 between $10000.01 and $25000 0.12% over $25000	Yes	Yes	ASX, US international
IG Trading	$5 or 0.05% on Australian shares $0.7% exchange fee for US and international shares	Yes	Custodial model: IG shares registered in CHESS under Citicorp	ASX, US international
NAB Trade	$9.95 fee for trades up to $1000 $14.95 between $1000.01 and $5000 $19.95 fee for trades between $5000.01 and $20000 0.11% trade value for trades above $20000	Yes	Yes	ASX, US international
Pearler	$6.50 flat fee You can also prepay your credits and pay $5.50 instead	Yes	Yes	ASX, US

App	Brokerage fees	Autoinvest?	CHESS sponsored?	Markets
SelfWealth	$9.50 flat fee	Can have target portfolio but no autoinvest features at the moment	Yes	ASX, US Hong Kong
Sharesies	1.9% transaction fee Capped at US$5 for US shares $6 for Australian Shares NZ$25 for NZ Shares	Yes: DIY, responsible and global orders	No	NZ, ASX, US
Stake	$3 or 0.01% of trades over $30 000	No	Yes	ASX, US
Superhero	$2 brokerage for all trades up to $20 000 or 0.01% for trades above $20 000 US$2 brokerage for all trades up to US$20 000 or 0.01% for trades above US$20 000	Yes	No	ASX, US

Note: Prices are accurate as of March 2025 but are subject to change. Only brokerage fees are included in the table; other fees may apply, so be sure to check this. All prices in AUD unless stated otherwise.

Step 3: Choose what to invest in

Time for the fun part: deciding what to buy. There are two types of investments to know about:

- Defensive investments: These are low risk, low return (think savings accounts or term deposits), and are best for short-term goals (up to three years).

- Growth investments: These are higher risk, higher return (like ETFs, shares or property), and are great for long-term goals (five or more years).

Pro tip: It's a good idea to start with ETFs. ETFs are kind of like the party mix bag of lollies. So instead of just buying one type of lolly, you can get mix of different ones. ETFs are the same, instead of buying just one stock, you get a mix of different companies in the one investment. They are low cost, diversified and way less risky than betting on a single company.

ETF portfolio options

Investing doesn't need to be complicated; you actually only need one or two ETFs in your portfolio. Here are some examples of super simple ETF portfolio combos:

- VAS + VGS: Covers both Australian and international markets without overlapping.
- VTS + VEU + VAS: This trio captures the US market and the rest of the world, including Australia.
- FAIR + VESG: This pair is a great start for those wanting ethical investing options.
- VDHG: This is an all-in-one diversified ETF.
- DZZF: Basically an ethical version of VDHG.

Step 4: Choose how much to invest

So now you're ready to dip your toes into investing, you're probably wondering how much to invest. A good rule of thumb is to keep your brokerage fees lower than 1 per cent of your total investment amount. For example, if the brokerage fee for your investing app is $10, then it's a good idea to invest at least $1000 so your brokerage fee is less than 1 per cent of the total amount.

And of course, the more you invest, the lower your brokerage fees are, as a percentage of how much you invest. So, for example, if you have a $10 brokerage fee, and you invest $2000 instead, then the brokerage fee would only be 0.5 per cent of the total amount.

Step 5: Automate your investing

Consistency is key. You could set up automatic deposits to invest the same amount every month — no effort required. Here's how to make it work: Pick a monthly amount (e.g., $1000), and invest regularly into an ETF. Then let the app do its thing. It's a 'set it and forget it' slow cooker, but for your money.

Step 6: Keep an eye on your money

Tracking your investments is important but it doesn't have to be boring. Many of the investing apps listed have their own in-built tax tools, or you could use an external platform like Sharesight to do it for you (FYI: this is not an ad, just wanted to mention this tool!).

It's important to track things such as:

- Dividends: These are the profits of companies, that some companies like to give to their shareholders (kind of like a thank you).
- Taxes: If you sell your investments for a profit, you'll need to pay tax on the capital gain. One thing to note though, is that there's 50 per cent capital gains tax discount if you hold onto your shares for longer than 12 months. It's one of the ways the government likes to reward long-term investors.

Compound interest: Why building wealth gets easier over time

Let's take you back to when Pablo and I were saving for our first home. That first $100 000 felt like a never-ending uphill battle.

We did everything we could to speed things up—renting out our garage, taking on side hustles, making websites on the side and cutting back wherever we could. Every dollar felt like it required *so much effort* to save.

Fast forward a few years and now our net worth can increase effortlessly without us even thinking about it.

The difference is *compound interest*.

Why your first $100 000 is the hardest (and why it gets easier)

There's something *magical* that happens when you hit your first $100 000 milestone—it's like the financial version of levelling up in a video game. The first level is tough, but once you get past it, things start happening faster.

When you start, you're the one working hard for your money. But once you invest, your money starts working for you. And the more you have invested, the faster it grows.

Let's break it down with real numbers (below, and figure 8.1). If you're autoinvesting $1000 a month with an 8 per cent annual return, the time it would take to reach each milestone would be:

- $100 000 → 6 years and 5 months (77 months)
- $200 000 → 4 years and 3 months (51 months)
- $300 000 → 3 years and 2 months (38 months)
- $400 000 → 2 years and 6 months (30 months)
- $500 000 → 2 years and 1 month (25 months)
- $600 000 → 1 year and 10 months (22 months)
- $700 000 → 1 year and 7 months (19 months)
- $800 000 → 1 year and 4 months (16 months)
- $900 000 → 1 year and 3 months (15 months)
- $1 000 000 → 1 year and 2 months (14 months)

Invest with confidence

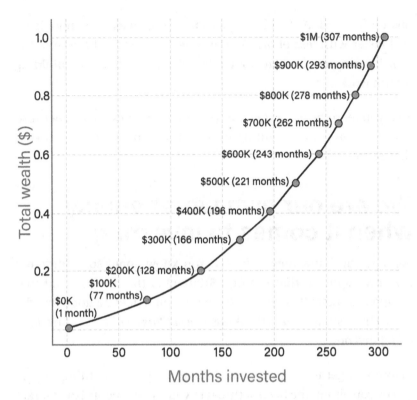

Figure 8.1: Compound interest growth: Investing $1000 per month at 8 per cent annual return

Every extra $100 000 takes less time because your investments are now earning money on their own.

If you're just getting started and it feels like it's taking *forever* to build wealth, trust the process. It won't always be this hard. The hardest part is getting started, but once you reach that first milestone, your money starts working harder than you do.

The takeaway: Wealth building is like a snowball

Think of compound interest like rolling a snowball down a hill. At first, it's tiny, and you have to put in the effort to shape it and push it forward. As it rolls, it picks up more snow, growing bigger and faster with less effort. By the time it's near the bottom of the hill, it's massive and unstoppable. This is exactly how building wealth works.

So if you're in the early stages of your journey, stick with it, because one day, your money will be making more money than you ever thought possible.

We are our own worst enemy when it comes to investing

So, now you know how to invest. You know about some different investing options, that the first $100 000 is the hardest, and that compound interest is your best friend. You're feeling good, maybe even a little smug. You're thinking, *I've got this wealth-building thing all figured out.*

Before you get too comfortable, let me tell you something no one warns you about: the biggest threat to your investments isn't market crashes, recessions or even global pandemics.

It's *you*. Your brain. Your emotions. Your panic reflex.

And I know this because I've been there.

Let me take you back to March 2020, aka *the month the entire world lost its mind.*

Pablo and I had been investing for a few years at this point. We were feeling pretty confident. We had a solid strategy. We understood long-term investing. And then... BAM! The news was a disaster.

Everywhere we looked:

- Stock markets in freefall!
- Global recession incoming!

- Unprecedented pandemic!
- People are panic-buying toilet paper!

We were glued to our screens, watching red numbers flash across the market like some kind of horror movie. Stocks were plummeting: the S&P 500 crashed over 30 per cent in just a few weeks. People were losing jobs, businesses were closing overnight and the overall mood was *doom. Absolute doom.*

We had just moved into our first home and were working from home, witnessing this chaos unfold. It was scary as hell.

At that moment, we wanted to panic. Sell. Hoard cash. Maybe even stock up on beans and rice, because, at this rate, who knew if money would even *exist* next month?

Then, we took a deep breath and we remembered something important: *The stock market loves drama*

If there's one thing you need to know about investing, it's this:

- markets will drop
- markets will rise
- the news will always be dramatic.

But over the long term? Markets typically recover.

It won't always be a perfect 8 per cent return every year. Some years, you'll be up 20 per cent or more; other years, you might be down 30 per cent.

But the key to winning the investing game is just staying in the game.

Vanguard even put together an amazing index chart (find the link in the Resources chapter at the end of the book) that shows just how volatile the market is in the short term, but also how, in the long run, it trends upward.

Market crashes: A brief history of freak-outs (and recoveries)

Here's a fun list of times when investors thought the world was ending, and the market *still* bounced back:

- Black Monday (1987): The Dow crashed 22 per cent in one day — the worst one-day drop in history. The market recovered in two years.
- Dot-com bubble (2000): Tech stocks imploded, dropping 76 per cent. The market recovered within six years.
- Global financial crisis (2008): Markets crashed by more than 50 per cent but recovered within four years.
- COVID-19 crash (2020): The S&P 500 crashed 34 per cent in just a few weeks and recovered in six months.

But, it's still important to diversify

Now, this is not to say that every stock market recovers and bounces back quickly. It's been the case with the US, Australia and most of the world, but if you look to Japan, it look a lot longer for their stock market to recover.

So that's why it's a good idea to diversify your investments. The US and Australian stock markets have performed really well over the last 100 years, but nobody knows what the future holds or if that will continue. So diversifying your investments into different markets (e.g., different countries), and even different assets classes (such as cash, property, gold, bonds, or even crypto if that's your jam) is a good idea. We'll talk about property in the next chapter.

Key takeaways

- Keep it simple: The best investing strategy isn't flashy, it's consistent. Low-cost index funds and ETFs often outperform fancy, high-fee funds.

- Time > timing: Trying to time the market usually backfires. The real magic happens when you invest regularly and let time (and compound interest) do the heavy lifting.
- Save for short-term, invest for long-term: Use high-interest savings for goals within five years. For anything beyond that, investing will help your money grow faster.
- Handle the basics first: Before investing, make sure you've got an emergency fund (three to six months of expenses) and you've paid off any high-interest debt.
- Your brain is the biggest risk: Market crashes happen. Don't panic. The biggest threat to your wealth is emotional decision-making, not market dips.
- Compound interest is your superpower: Your first $100 000 is the hardest, but once your investments start earning for you, growth snowballs faster than you think.

In a nutshell

Now that you've unlocked the power of investing, you've got the foundation to build serious wealth. But what if you're ready to buy a property. Whether it's buying your first home, investing in real estate or just understanding if property is the right move for you, the next chapter will show you how to make property rewarding... without the overwhelm.

Chapter 9
Win the PROPERTY game

Buying our first home was *exciting*... in the same way that trying to assemble IKEA furniture is exciting. You start out optimistic, but somewhere along the way, the stress, confusion and occasional urge to cry kick in.

We didn't have a huge budget, so we were looking at one- and two-bedroom apartments, hoping to find something that didn't feel like a shoebox but also didn't require us to sell a kidney.

Then we found *the one*.

It was perfect — or so we thought.

A one-bedroom apartment, modern and sleek, with beautifully maintained courtyards. It had an island kitchen (which made me feel very 'celebrity chef'), an open living area and a balcony that overlooked a river. Not to mention, it was just a *seven-minute* walk to the train station — so close, yet far enough that we wouldn't hear announcements about delays every morning.

And the cherry on top was that there were two supermarkets nearby. *Two*. If one was out of stock on oat milk, we had options.

It ticked all the boxes *and* was within budget, which honestly felt like winning the lottery. The real estate agent, sensing our excitement, asked if we wanted to make an offer. We told him we'd think about it and went home, feeling like we were one step away from signing on the dotted line.

But then, I got a *feeling*.

You know when you meet someone who seems too nice, and your gut tells you to check if they've been on *A Current Affair*? That's what I felt about this apartment.

I decided to Google the developer. What I found was an absolute horror show. One article after another:

- 'Dodgy developer refuses to fix major building defects.'
- 'Apartments plagued with leaks and cracks. Owners left to pay massive repair bills.'
- 'Company directors disappear after pocketing millions.'

And then came the pièce de résistance: a full-on *exposé video*. The footage showed heartbroken owners dealing with wardrobe doors that wouldn't close, massive balcony cracks and water damage that looked like it belonged in an abandoned theme park.

The developers (who were nowhere to be found when owners needed urgent repairs) were very visible in another clip. A video surfaced of the owner of the construction company showing off the brand-new Lamborghini he had bought his wife.

I sat back in disbelief. We had almost handed over our life savings to these people.

Needless to say, we ran far away from that deal and instead bought an older two-bedroom apartment that needed a little love but at least wouldn't crumble around us.

Fast forward five years and, out of curiosity, I checked the price of that 'dream' one-bedroom apartment. It had dropped 40 per cent in value while our apartment had gone up 40 per cent.

This whole experience taught me one of the most valuable lessons of my life:

Always, always research the developer.

Sometimes, what looks like the perfect home is just an expensive disaster with a fresh coat of paint.

> ### What's coming up next...
>
> This chapter is your ultimate guide to making property rewarding, not stressful. Whether you're buying your first home or looking for an investment, we'll cover:
>
> - how to avoid property nightmares (like dodgy developers and hidden defects)
> - smart strategies to save for your deposit without sacrificing your lifestyle
> - the red flags to watch for when inspecting properties (so you don't get stuck with surprise costs)
> - how to think like an investor, even if you're buying something to live in
> - mortgage hacks to save thousands and pay off your loan faster
> - auction tips to help you stay cool and confident (no overbidding drama here).
>
> By the end of this chapter, you'll feel ready to navigate the property market like a pro — without the stress, confusion or regrets.

What kind of property are you after?

Before you start property hunting, it helps to get crystal clear on what you actually want.

Are you buying a home to live in? If so, is this your *forever* home, or just a stepping stone to something bigger and better? Or maybe you're looking for an investment property, one that can grow in value and make you money over time.

If you're buying a property to live in

If you're buying a home to live in, here's one thing to remember: your first home doesn't need to be perfect, it just needs to work for you.

When I bought my first home, it wasn't exactly giving luxury vibes. The oven didn't work, the kitchen cupboards were one gentle tug away from collapse, but you know what? It was a start. And a year later, we renovated, added value and turned it into something much better.

That home ended up being a stepping stone to buying the home we are in now: a bigger, nicer place that suits our needs much better.

So if your first home isn't your dream home, *that's okay*. Think of it as a launch pad, a way to get your foot in the market so you can upgrade later once you have more money.

Think like an investor (even if you're buying a home to live in)

Even if you're buying your home to live in, it pays to think like an investor.

- Location matters: Pick a place that's close to transport, shops, schools or other amenities.
- Quality matters: A well-built home will save you from future headaches (and costly repairs).

- Future value matters: A good property can grow in value, giving you options later.

But why does this matter? Buying smart sets you up for more financial flexibility. Down the track, you could use the equity in your home to upgrade to a bigger place or sell it for a good price when you're ready for your next move.

So while it's your home first, it can also be a powerful wealth-building tool if you buy right.

If you're buying a property as an investment

Investing in property isn't just about buying any place and hoping for the best, it's about making a strategic choice that will grow your wealth over time.

Before you sign anything, make sure you've done your homework on the:

- Suburb: Are there new developments, schools or infrastructure projects coming up?
- Vacancy rates: How easy will it be to find tenants?
- Rental yield: Will the rent cover your costs, or at least make a decent contribution?
- The property itself: Check for any hidden issues that could turn your investment into a money pit.

Apartments vs houses

A lot of people assume they *have* to buy an apartment because it's more affordable, but that's not always the best move.

Houses (especially in smaller cities or regional areas) have historically appreciated more than apartments. They also give you more land value, which can make a big difference in long-term growth.

If your goal is capital growth, it's worth exploring different markets rather than just looking at apartments in big cities.

Getting help from a buyer's agent

If you're not familiar with the area you're buying in — or just don't have the time to deep dive into property research — it could be worth hiring a buyer's agent.

Yes, their fees can be steep, but the right agent can:

- help you find properties that match your goals
- negotiate a better price (saving you thousands in the long run)
- avoid costly mistakes that many first-time investors make.

Think of it as an investment in expert guidance. It's an upfront cost that could save you a lot more in the long run.

Set a target

Once you have an idea on what type of property you're looking to buy, visit real estate websites and check recently sold properties in areas you like. This will give you a realistic idea of what's achievable and help you set a savings target. Remember, your first property is just the beginning of your journey.

You don't need a 20 per cent deposit

Something that I wish I knew when we were buying our first home, is that you don't actually need a 20 per cent deposit to buy your first home.

You can buy a home with as little as a 5 or 10 per cent deposit but, typically, if you do have less than a 20 per cent deposit you may have to pay for lenders' mortgage insurance (LMI). This insurance is for the bank.

But here's where it gets cool — depending on where you live, there may be some first home buyer schemes you could take advantage of that could reduce or eliminate this extra cost. In Australia, schemes such as the First Home Loan Deposit Scheme allow you to buy with as little as a 5 per cent deposit without paying LMI. Of course, there are conditions, but it can be a game-changer for first-time buyers.

Saving for your deposit without sacrificing everything

Saving for a home can feel like climbing Everest, but it doesn't have to be all scrimping and no smashed avo on toast. Here's how you can boost your savings *without* feeling like you're living on two-minute noodles.

First Home Buyers Super Saver

Another thing that I wish I did was look into the First Home Super Saver (FHSS). If you're in Australia, this scheme allows you to turbocharge your savings while cutting down your tax bill. Basically, how it works is, you get to save for your first home in your superannuation, and then withdraw these extra savings when you're ready to buy. Of course, there are conditions, but it can be a game-changer for first-time buyers.

Here's how it works.

You start by making extra contributions to your super. You can salary sacrifice before-tax (concessional contributions) or make after-tax (non-concessional) contributions. You can contribute up to $15 000 per financial year and withdraw up to $50 000 total. Your employer sets up the salary sacrifice (or you can make voluntary payments).

Your take-home pay is slightly lower because you're putting more into super, but since concessional contributions are taxed at 15 per cent instead of your usual income tax rate, you could save big on tax.

When you're ready to buy, apply to withdraw your FHSS savings plus any earnings through the Australian Tax Office (ATO) — this takes time, so plan ahead. You'll pay tax on the withdrawal, but you get a

30 per cent tax offset, meaning if you're in the 30 per cent tax bracket, you won't owe anything extra.

Why it's worth considering

- Faster savings growth: Super investments can help your deposit grow more than a regular savings account.
- Lower tax bill: Contributions are taxed at 15 per cent instead of your usual income tax rate, which could be much higher.
- Great for disciplined savings: Since it's locked away, you won't be tempted to dip into it for a spontaneous shopping spree.

Things to keep in mind

- You must apply for a determination from the ATO before signing a contract to buy a home.
- The money won't hit your account overnight; withdrawals can take 15 to 25 business days.
- Not all super funds allow FHSS withdrawals, so check with yours first.
- You need to live in the home for at least six months within the first 12 months after purchase.
- This is a bit more hassle to set up than a regular savings account, so see if it's worth it for you.

Table 9.1 breaks down the numbers into more detail by looking at FHSS vs a regular savings account.

Table 9.1: FHSS vs. savings account

Scenario	FHSS	Regular bank savings
Annual contribution	$10 000	$10 000
Tax rate (before FHSS)	30 per cent	30 per cent
Tax paid	$1500 (super tax rate 15 per cent)	$3000 (income tax rate 30 per cent)
Amount saved per year	$8500	$7000
After five years	$42 500 (+ earnings)	$35 000

That's an extra $7500 saved, just from tax savings alone!

Bottom line

If you're a first-home buyer, the FHSS scheme is worth looking into. It's a smart way to save faster, pay less tax and grow your deposit without feeling the pinch as much. But it is a lot more hassle to set up, so have a think to see if it's right for you.

Saving in a high-interest savings account

A high-interest savings account can supercharge your home deposit savings. Instead of leaving your cash in an account that barely earns interest, you can put it somewhere that actually grows!

Why a high-interest savings account?

Let's say you're saving $10 000 per year for a home deposit. Table 9.2 shows how much you could have after five years, depending on where you park your cash.

Table 9.2: Interest rates compared

Savings strategy	Interest rate	Total after five years	Extra earned
High-interest savings account	5.5 per cent	$58 220	$8220 in interest
Regular savings account	2 per cent	$52 040	$2040 in interest

That's a $6180 difference, just by choosing the right account!

How to find the best account

- Look for an account with no monthly fees.
- Check for bonus interest conditions (some accounts require a certain number of deposits or no withdrawals) and make sure you can meet these bonus interest rate conditions easily.
- Compare different banks and digital banks — some online banks offer higher rates than the big four.
- Make sure they are government-backed and insured with the financial claims scheme. The government insures

deposits of up $250 000 per account holder per authorised deposit-taking institution (ADI). You can check out a list of government-approved lenders through APRA (the full URL is in the Resources chapter at the back of the book).

Extra tips on how to maximise your savings

- Automate it: Set up a dedicated high-interest savings account just for your deposit.
- Break it down: Need to save $10 000 in a year? That's just $27.40 a day, roughly the price of a coffee and a cheap lunch.
- Review your spending: Audit your subscriptions, phone plans, gym memberships, anything that's quietly draining your account. If you don't use it, cancel it.

Investing for your home deposit

Another option is investing your savings instead of leaving them in cash. This is what we did; we invested in ETFs to grow our home deposit.

When the market is doing well, this strategy can boost your savings, helping you reach your goal faster. But there's a catch: the stock market is unpredictable. If there's a downturn right when you need to withdraw, your deposit could shrink instead of grow. This means you could see:

- Higher potential returns: Historically, ETFs and shares have outperformed regular savings accounts over the long term.
- Higher risk: If you plan to buy within five years, there's always a chance the market drops at the wrong time, leaving you with less than you started with.

Should you invest your home deposit?

- If you have a longer timeframe (five or more years) before buying, investing could be a great way to grow your deposit.
- If you're okay with market ups and downs and won't need to access the money urgently this could be a great option.

- If you plan to buy within a few years, a high-interest savings account or the FHSS may be a safer bet.

Navigating mortgages with this simple trick

Your mortgage is one of the biggest financial commitments you'll make, so getting it right is crucial. At first, I hesitated to use a mortgage broker, but it turned out to be one of the best decisions. Brokers are paid by the banks, so their services are free for you and me. And they can give you a variety of different loan options and help you secure the best deal.

Hot tip: Get pre-approved for your mortgage before you start house hunting. It gives you a competitive edge and signals to agents that you're serious.

Getting a buyer's agent for an auction

If you've ever been to an auction, you'll know it can also feel like a high-stakes poker game where everyone else knows the rules except you.

One of my childhood friends recently went through this experience, and let's just say, auctions are not for the faint-hearted.

They had their eye on a beautiful place and were really keen. On auction day, they showed up early, partly to get a good spot, but mostly to scope out the competition. Who else was bidding? Were they serious buyers or just there for the drama?

Then the real estate agent arrived — all smiles, full of energy — ready to put on a show.

The auction begins... awkwardly. 'We'll start the bidding at [insert a number that makes you gulp]'.

Silence.

My friend looks around. Nobody moves. Not a single paddle is raised.

'Okay, folks, let's get things going! Who wants to make an offer?'

More silence.

Now, at this point, you'd think the agent might lower the price to spark some interest. But instead, they turn to my friend and basically say, 'Well, since you're here, why don't you start us off?'

Hesitant, but eager, my friend nods and makes an offer.

'We have a bid!' The real estate agent barely acknowledges it before pushing back. 'Sorry, too low. We need to start higher.'

My friend, already emotionally invested, reluctantly agrees.

'Alright, new bid! Who's next?'

...Crickets.

No one else bids. Now things start getting awkward.

The real estate agent is practically pleading with the crowd, walking up to people, making small talk, trying to convince them to throw in an offer. But still — nothing.

And that's when something *really* strange happens.

'The vendor has placed a bid!'

Wait. What?

Yep, the owner (or as real estate agents call them, 'the vendor') made a bid on their own property.

This is known as a vendor bid, and it's basically a way to push the price up artificially when no one else is biting. My friend was confused. The bidding had been at one level, and now suddenly the price had jumped significantly — even though no real buyers have put their hands up.

The agent tells them, 'You'll need to go higher if you want this place'.

At this point, my friend had to make a call: walk away and risk losing the home or negotiate and secure it.

After some back and forth, they ended up securing the property at a price they were comfortable with — not a total win, but not a terrible deal either.

The auction trap first-time buyers fall into

This is a classic situation that first-home buyers face all the time. Auctions are high-pressure, fast-moving and designed to play on emotions. If you're not careful, you might end up bidding against a vendor bid, which is designed to push the price up; feeling pressured to increase your offer, even when there's no real competition; overpaying in the heat of the moment, because no one wants to lose an auction.

This is where having a buyer's agent can make a difference.

How we used a buyer's agent at our auction

When Pablo and I were buying our second home, we knew we didn't want to risk overbidding or getting caught up in the excitement, so we hired a buyer's agent to bid for us at the auction.

Best. Decision. Ever.

And here's why — they know:

- how to read the room, spotting serious bidders vs people just there for the show

- when to slow things down: instead of jumping in with big bids, they nudged it up by small increments at a time
- how to keep emotions out of it — unlike us, they weren't attached to the house. No excitement, no nerves, just strategy.

If we had bid ourselves, we easily could have overpaid by getting caught up in the auction energy.

Should you get a buyer's agent for an auction?

If you're a first-home buyer, consider hiring a buyer's agent to bid on your behalf.

- Cost: Usually $400 to $1000 (depending on the agent and auction).
- Potential savings: Could be thousands just by avoiding overbidding.

A buyer's agent isn't necessary for everyone, but if you're feeling nervous about an auction, or just don't want to deal with the mind games real estate agents play, it's something worth considering.

Real estate vs stocks: What's the better investment?

It's one of the biggest debates in investing: should you invest in property or stocks?

After investing in both, here's what I've learned: They each have their pros and cons, and, honestly, you don't even have to choose — you can do both!

It all comes down to your personal preferences, risk tolerance and financial goals. Let's break it down.

Investing in real estate: What it's really like

There's something about owning property that feels secure. It's tangible. You can live in it, rent it out or renovate it. Plus, real estate has one of the biggest advantages in investing: leverage.

With property, you don't need to pay the full amount upfront. With a 10 to 20 per cent deposit, you can control a much larger asset, allowing for higher potential returns over time.

If you pick the right property, in the right area and hold it for long enough, you can build serious wealth through capital growth and rental income. That being said, real estate isn't all passive income and capital gains.

- It's expensive: Buying property comes with stamp duty, legal fees, maintenance, council rates, insurance and interest repayments.
- It's a long-term game: Unlike stocks, you can't just sell a bedroom if you need extra cash. Property is illiquid, meaning it takes time (and costs money) to sell.
- Markets fluctuate: Property prices don't always go up, and interest rates can make repayments more expensive.

Pros

- Leverage: Control a large asset with a smaller deposit.
- Equity growth: You can borrow against your property to invest in more.
- Rental income: Tenants can help cover your mortgage.
- Tax benefits: Depreciation, negative gearing and deductions.

Cons

- Expensive upfront costs: Stamp duty, legal fees, maintenance and interest all add up.
- Illiquidity: Selling takes time and money.

- Market risks: Property prices aren't guaranteed to rise.
- Management effort: Tenants, maintenance and ongoing costs require time and attention.

Investing in stocks: What it's really like

Investing in stocks (shares, ETFs, index funds) is one of the easiest ways to build wealth. Unlike real estate, you don't need a huge deposit or a loan, you can start with as little as $1000 and build your portfolio over time.

Stocks are also much more liquid than property. If you need money, you can sell your shares instantly (unlike selling a house, which can take months).

One of the biggest advantages of stocks is compound growth. If you reinvest dividends and let your investments grow over time, the returns can snowball massively.

Pros
- Low barrier to entry: Start with as little as $1000.
- High liquidity: Buy and sell instantly.
- Compound growth: Let your money grow over time.
- No maintenance required: There are no tenants, no repairs, no interest repayments.

Cons
- Market volatility: Prices fluctuate daily.
- Requires emotional discipline: Many people panic and sell too soon.
- More difficult to leverage: You can't borrow against stocks as easily as property.

Which one is better?

Both are great options, and it all depends on your goals and what type of investor you are.

- If you want leverage, long-term stability and rental income → real estate might be for you.
- If you want flexibility, easy diversification and passive growth → stocks might be the better choice.

But here's the thing: you don't have to choose. You can invest in both! And, even better, by doing both you can diversify your assets too.

Plenty of investors use real estate to build wealth and stocks to create passive income. Others start with stocks because they require less capital, then move into real estate later.

There's no one-size-fits-all answer — just the investment strategy that works best for you.

The hidden costs of buying a home

Owning a home isn't just about making mortgage repayments, there are plenty of extra costs that can sneak up on you if you're not prepared.

When I bought my first home, I *thought* I was ready. Then the unexpected expenses started rolling in: council rates, maintenance, strata fees, insurance... Suddenly, home ownership didn't feel as cheap as I thought.

To help you budget properly, here's a breakdown of all the hidden costs (with rough estimates of how much they might set you back).

Upfront costs (before you even get the keys)

Buying a property comes with a stack of once-off costs that you'll need to budget for before settlement day (see table 9.3).

Table 9.3: Calculating the upfront costs of buying property

Cost	What it covers	Approximate cost
Deposit	Typically 10 to 20 per cent of the property price. Some lenders accept as low as 5 per cent with LMI.	$50 000–$150 000+ (for a $500 000–$750 000 home)
Stamp duty	State tax on property purchases (varies by state and first-home buyer exemptions may apply).	$0–$30 000+
Lenders' mortgage insurance (LMI)	If your deposit is less than 20 per cent, you may need to pay LMI (varies by lender).	$5000–$30 000+
Legal/ conveyancing fees	Covers the legal work involved in transferring property ownership.	$1000–$3000
Building and pest inspection	Essential for checking for structural issues, termites or hidden damage.	$300–$800
Mortgage application fees	Some banks charge a one-off fee for setting up your home loan.	$0–$1000
Moving costs	Hiring removalists, renting a truck or bribing friends with pizza to help you pack and move!	$500–$3000

How much should you budget?

If you're buying a $750 000 home, you'll likely need $60 000 to $100 000 upfront (including your deposit, fees and inspections).

Ongoing costs (the stuff you pay every year)

Once you own the home, there are a bunch of recurring costs that come with it. Table 9.4 details what you need to consider.

Table 9.4: Calculating the ongoing costs of buying property

Cost	What it covers	Approximate cost per year
Mortgage interest	The amount of interest you pay on your loan (varies based on your loan size and rate)	$20 000–$50 000
Home insurance	Covers damage from fires, storms and other unexpected disasters	$1000–$3000

Cost	What it covers	Approximate cost per year
Council rates	Charged by your local council for rubbish collection, roads, etc.	$1500–$3500
Water rates	Charges for water usage and sewage services	$500–$1500
Strata fees (if in an apartment/unit)	Covers building maintenance, insurance and shared spaces	$2000–$8000
General maintenance and repairs	Fixing things like plumbing, electrical, leaks, wear and tear	$2000–$5000
Land tax (if applicable)	Some states charge tax on land value if it exceeds a threshold	Varies by state

Surprise maintenance costs

Even if your home is in great condition, unexpected repairs can pop up at any time. A few real-life examples:

- A leaky roof could cost $5000+ to fix.
- If your hot water system dies, that's easily another $1500 to $3000.
- Or if you get hit with a major plumbing issue, that could be $2000+, depending on the damage.

How much to budget?

A good rule of thumb is to set aside 1 per cent of your property's value per year for maintenance. So for a $750 000 home, you should budget $7500 annually just for repairs and upkeep.

Exit costs (when you sell or rent it out)

If you're planning to sell in the future, there are exit costs too. It's not as simple as just cashing in on your equity. If you're planning to sell a property, table 9.5 (overleaf) shows the exit costs you'll need to factor in.

Table 9.5: Calculating your exit costs on a property

Cost	What it covers	Approximate cost
Real estate agent fees	Agents take a 1.5 to 3 per cent commission when selling your home	$10 000–$25 000+
Marketing fees	Photos, online listings, signage and advertising	$1000–$5000
Capital gains tax (if investment property)	Tax on profits from selling an investment property	Varies based on income

How much to budget?

If you're selling a $750 000 home, expect to pay $15 000 to $30 000+ in agent and marketing fees.

Your turn: Create a budget for these costs

The best way to avoid financial shocks is to plan ahead.

- Make a spreadsheet of every possible cost: upfront, ongoing and exit costs.
- Add buffer savings: things will break, and it's better to be prepared.
- Shop around for lower costs: compare lenders, insurers and service providers.

Inspect, negotiate and inspect again

Whether you're buying your first home or an investment, due diligence is key:

- Inspect thoroughly: If it's a house, get a building and pest inspection. For apartments, review the strata report to avoid nasty surprises.

- Negotiate smartly: Use minor defects to your advantage. Aim for a win-win deal because low-ball offers can backfire.
- Get legal help: Always have a solicitor review contracts. It's tempting to skim, but those fine details can save you big time.

How to pay off your mortgage faster

A mortgage is usually a 30-year commitment, but that doesn't mean you have to wait 30 years to be debt-free. Small, strategic changes can help you pay it off years earlier and save tens (or even hundreds) of thousands in interest.

Here are two simple but powerful ways to do it.

1. Switch from monthly to weekly or fortnightly payments

Most people pay their mortgage monthly because that's what the bank suggests. But did you know that switching to fortnightly or weekly payments can cut years off your loan?

How it works

There are 12 months in a year, meaning you make 12 mortgage payments annually.

If you switch to fortnightly payments, you'll make 26 payments a year (since there are 52 weeks in a year, divided by two).

This means you're effectively making one extra month's payment every year (13 rather than 12) — without even realising it! But if your brain hurts and you don't fully get it, don't worry because I'm going to break down the numbers...

Let's say your mortgage repayment is $3000 per month.

- Paying monthly: $3000 × 12 = $36 000 per year
- Paying fortnightly: $1500 (half the monthly amount) × 26 = $39 000 per year

That's an extra $3000 going towards your loan every year, just by changing your repayment schedule.

How much can this save you?

On a $500 000 loan at 6 per cent interest over 30 years, switching to fortnightly payments could cut four to five years off your loan and save over $100 000 in interest.

Action step: Ask your lender to switch your repayments to weekly or fortnightly to start reducing your loan faster.

2. Use an offset account to slash interest

An offset account is like a secret weapon for paying off your mortgage faster. It's a normal transaction account linked to your home loan, but any money sitting in it reduces the interest charged on your mortgage.

How it works

Instead of earning 1 to 2 per cent interest in a regular savings account (which is also taxed), putting your savings into an offset account, offsets the loan balance — so you only pay interest on the remaining amount. And since you're saving interest, not earning interest, it's not taxed.

Here's an example to explain. Let's say you have:

- $500 000 mortgage at 6 per cent interest over 30 years
- $50 000 sitting in an offset account

That $50 000 offsets your loan balance, so instead of paying interest on $500 000, you only pay interest on $450 000.

How much can this save you?

You could pay off your mortgage five years earlier, and save around $194 934 in interest.

How to maximise your offset account

Consider keeping your emergency fund in your offset account. As we discussed on page 136, it's a good idea to have three to six months of living expenses saved in cash for emergencies. Rather than keep this money in a savings account, put it to work offsetting your mortgage and saving you money.

Your turn: Put it all on paper

Take ten minutes to write down:

- your homeownership goal (live in or investment?)
- your budget and deposit strategy
- one action you'll take this month to move closer to buying.

By making your first home purchase strategic and fun, you'll not only get into the market sooner, but you'll set yourself up for financial success in the long run.

Key takeaways

Buying your first home can feel overwhelming, but it doesn't have to be. By breaking it down into simple, strategic steps, you can enjoy the process and make smarter financial choices.

Let's tie it all together.

Focus on your goals

- What kind of property do you actually want? Is this a stepping stone, a forever home or an investment? Define your why before diving in.
- Set a savings target: Use real estate listings to check realistic prices so you know exactly what you're working towards.

Use the right strategies

- Don't wait for a 20 per cent deposit: You can buy with 5 to 10 per cent and take advantage of first-home buyer schemes.
- Boost your savings: Use high-interest savings accounts, FHSS, or even ETFs (if your timeline allows).
- Think like an investor: Even if you're buying to live in, location, quality and future value matter.

Navigate smartly

- Auctions can be intense: Consider hiring a buyer's agent to help you win without overbidding.
- Do your due diligence: Always research developers, get a building inspection and check for hidden costs.
- Save on your mortgage: Use an offset account, switch to fortnightly payments and make extra repayments when possible.

In a nutshell

Buying property isn't just about finding a place to live, it's one of the biggest financial moves you'll ever make. But with the right strategies, it can be both rewarding and fun. The key is to focus on long-term value, trust your instincts and stay informed.

Now that you've got the foundations of property covered, it's time to shift gears. In the next chapter, we'll dive into the fun in tracking your wealth, because what's the point of building wealth if you don't get to watch it grow? Let's make tracking your money feel as satisfying as hitting a new level in your favourite game. Get ready to feel empowered, motivated and addicted to your own progress.

Chapter 10
TRACK your wealth for fun

I'm writing this chapter while squished into an economy seat on a flight to Thailand, sandwiched between my partner Pablo, our baby and a stranger who has already fallen asleep *on my shoulder*. We *tried* to book a points business class flight, but the universe had other plans. Even our upgrade request was brutally rejected.

So here we are, crammed into economy, feeling slightly bummed that we're not sipping champagne in lie-flat seats. But just as I'm settling in for my eight-hour battle with a rogue armrest, I hear a girl behind me exclaim, 'OMG, they have screens!' She turns to her friend, absolutely buzzing with excitement.

In that moment, I had a realisation — I used to be that girl. The first time Pablo and I flew on a full-service airline, we were *obsessed* with the screen, the food and snack service, the tiny (but free!) water bottles. It felt so *fancy* compared to the no-frills budget flights we usually took, where the only 'entertainment' was watching people fight over overhead luggage space and the seat recliner.

What changed? It wasn't the experience—it was *me*. That's the tricky thing about money. We're wired to always want *more*, to level up, to get bigger, better, fancier things. It's called the hedonic treadmill—the idea that we adapt *way* too quickly to upgrades, and what once felt like luxury becomes the new normal. Win the lottery? You'll be thrilled... for a little while. Lose out on a business class upgrade? You'll be grumpy, but only temporarily. Humans are *great* at normalising both wins and losses.

And that's why tracking your wealth is *so important*. Because if you don't track how far you've come, you'll *never* feel like you're making progress. You'll always be chasing the next thing, forgetting that past you would be shook by how rich present you is.

What's coming up next...

In this chapter, we're diving into the *real* secret to staying motivated on your wealth-building journey: tracking your progress. Think of it as your personal financial leaderboard: keeping score, celebrating wins and staying pumped.

You'll discover:

- how to calculate your net worth (without having a meltdown if it's not where you want it to be yet)
- what to track beyond just your bank balance, because your wealth is more than numbers on a screen
- fun ways to make tracking addictive, like turning it into a game that gives you a little dopamine hit every time you check in
- why celebrating small wins matters (hint: it's scientifically proven to keep you motivated)
- how to avoid burnout by zooming out and seeing the bigger picture when progress feels slow.

> If you've ever felt like you're working hard but not getting anywhere, this chapter will change that. Let's make tracking your wealth feel as satisfying as hitting a new high score.

So how do you actually keep track of where you're going with your finances?

One of the best ways to see where you're currently at with your finances is to calculate your net worth. Pablo and I started tracking our net worth back when it was in the negatives (because of our student loans), and we've been tracking it every month ever since. It's incredibly motivating to see how it can improve over time.

What is net worth?

Your net worth is simply the value of what you own (assets) minus what you owe (liabilities).

- Assets = things that make you money or hold value: your stock portfolio, retirement savings, cash savings or property.
- Liabilities = debts that you owe: your mortgage, student loans/HECS, credit card balances or car loan.

Don't stress if it's negative, especially if you're doing it for the first time

If you're calculating your net worth for the first time and it's in the negative, that's totally okay. Most people start in the red (hello, student debt). Tracking your net worth isn't about perfection, it's about progress.

Sample net worth calculation

Table 10.1 shows an example:

Table 10.1: a sample net worth calculation

Assets	Value	Liabilities	Value
Savings	$10 000	Mortgage	~$400 000
Investments (shares and ETFs)	$20 000	Credit card debt	~$2000
Superannuation	$50 000		
Home value	$500 000		
Total	**$580 000**	**Total**	**~$402 000**
Net worth calculation:		$580 000−$402 000 = $178 000	

Over time, the goal is to increase your assets, decrease your liabilities and watch that net worth number grow!

How to find your net worth

It's not always easy to track down all the figures that make up your net worth, but there are some specific places you can go and tools you can use to start putting together your net worth snapshot.

Banking apps

Don't underestimate your bank's app. It's a handy tool for quickly checking the cash you have in your accounts, and your debt if you have any mortgages. Plus, it helps you stay on top of your spending and savings goals.

Stock and crypto investing apps

If you're investing in the stock market or in crypto, checking your investing app can be a fantastic way to monitor progress. There are so many out there, each with pros and cons (refer back to Chapter 8 for some recommended apps to get you started).

Tax-reporting tools

If you have multiple investment apps, you can connect it to a tool like Sharesight that can give you your full investment portfolio in the one place. It's also great for calculating returns and even helps with tax reporting too.

Retirement balances

Don't forget about your retirement savings, like superannuation in Australia. This is another key part of your financial journey, even if you're not at the age where you can access it yet. Checking in on this regularly can be super motivating, as the balance grows over time with contributions and market performance.

Property value

If you own your own home, or have investment properties, chances are quite a big amount of your net worth is tied up in your property equity. You can find the value of your home by checking out websites like Zillow in the US or domain.com.au or realestate.com.au in Australia, which give your property's estimated market value. But you can also do your own valuation by looking at comparable, recently sold properties in a similar location. If you want to be super accurate, you could even get a professional valuation done every so often (although this may come with an extra cost).

Your turn: Calculate your net worth

Calculate your net worth by filling in Table 10.2 (overleaf). And don't worry if it's not exactly where you'd like it to be initially, it's all about seeing where you're at now and making progress.

Table 10.2: Calculating your worth

Assets	Value
Savings	$
Stocks	$
Superannuation	$
Home value	$
Gold	$
Crypto	$
Total assets	$
Liabilities	**Value**
Mortgage	$
Credit card debt	$
Personal loans	$
Car loans	$
Total liabilities	$
Net worth calculation (assets minus liabilities)	$

Free net worth tracker

And if tracking your net worth on paper doesn't work for you, we've made it super easy for you with our free net worth tracker (investwithqueenie.com/net-worth-tracker). Download the tracker, pop in your own numbers and let it calculate everything automatically. Tracking your wealth has never been this simple — or this fun!

How often should you track your net worth?

Imagine you're a pilot flying from Sydney to Bangkok. You take off, feeling great, but a tiny 1 per cent shift off course could mean you end up in India instead. Yikes.

That's why pilots don't just *hope* they land in the right place, they constantly check their instruments, adjust for wind changes and make tiny course corrections to stay on track.

Your financial journey is the same. Life throws curveballs: unexpected bills, job changes, market dips. If you're not checking in, even small missteps can compound over time. But the good news is that *tiny tweaks now prevent massive corrections later.*

Here's the thing: Just like pilots don't panic over every spot of turbulence, so you don't need to stress over every small dip in your net worth. It's normal for it to fluctuate. The goal isn't *perfection*, it's progress.

So whether you check in weekly, monthly or quarterly, make sure you're checking in. Your dream financial destination is waiting; just don't forget to adjust your course along the way.

So, how often should you check it? Well, that depends on your personality:

- If you love data and tracking every move → weekly might give you that dopamine hit.
- If you want a good balance between motivation and not overthinking it → monthly is a solid sweet spot (this is what I do).
- If you prefer a more chill approach → quarterly or even half-yearly can still work, as long as you're checking in enough to stay on track.

Budgeting tools

We spoke about budgeting in Chapter 5, but it's definitely worth checking in regularly to see how you're staying on top of your spending, saving and investing. I've created a tool called Billroo (find it at billroo.com) that can help you budget, but there are a lot of other great budgeting apps out there too.

Keeping motivated on the journey

A few years ago, I had *the* best boss ever. You know, the kind of boss who actually makes you look forward to Monday mornings? (I know — rare.)

She was a powerhouse at setting goals, and every week we'd have 1:1 check-ins to track our progress. But here's what made her legendary: whenever we hit a milestone (big or small), she would book something fun for the team.

I'm not talking about extravagant, over-the-top yacht parties (though I wouldn't have said no to that). Sometimes it was as simple as a team lunch, or knocking off early to go for a massage. Other times, it was a proper celebration: fancy dinners, even surprise activities.

At first, I thought, *Wow, this is nice!* But then I realised — this wasn't just about having fun; it was strategic.

Treat yourself like a high-performing employee

Think about it — if you were managing a team, would you just throw money at them and expect them to stay motivated? No way.

A great leader keeps their team engaged by setting clear goals, celebrating progress and making work rewarding. So, do the same for yourself! Be your own best boss.

Just like we discussed in Chapter 7 about celebrating small wins, you can apply these treats to the progress you make in your financial journey.

Zoom out to avoid burnout

Ever been stuck in traffic, creeping forward at snail speed, convinced you'll never actually get where you're going? Then suddenly, after what feels like *forever*, the road clears and you're flying down the highway?

That's exactly what wealth-building feels like.

Some months, you're cruising—saving heaps, smashing your financial goals, feeling like a money *genius*. Other months? A surprise bill, a car repair or a market dip throws you off, and you feel like you're barely moving.

Spoiler alert: You're still making progress.

If you only focus on the day-to-day, it's easy to feel frustrated. But if you zoom out and look at your progress over three, six or 12 months, you'll see the bigger picture.

Wealth-building isn't a straight road—it's full of detours, speed bumps and slow downs. But as long as you're still heading in the right direction, you're *winning*.

So when you hit a rough patch, don't panic. Take a deep breath, check your financial map and keep going.

Key takeaways

- Track your net worth: Your net worth = what you own (assets) - what you owe (liabilities). It's the ultimate snapshot of your financial health.
- Progress over perfection: Don't stress if your net worth isn't where you want it to be. It's about growth, not perfection. Even starting in the negative is totally normal.
- Make it fun: Turn tracking into a game—use apps, spreadsheets or tools to see your progress and get that sweet dopamine hit.
- Check in regularly: Whether it's weekly, monthly or quarterly, consistent check-ins help you stay on course and catch any financial drift early.

- Celebrate the wins: Don't wait for 'big milestones'. Celebrate every step — whether it's saving your first $1000, paying off a credit card or hitting a new investment goal.
- Zoom out: Wealth-building isn't linear. There will be ups, downs and plateaus. But when you zoom out, you'll see just how far you've come.

In a nutshell

Calculating your net worth is one of the best ways to assess where you currently are at with your finances, and tracking it regularly can be incredibly motivating to see the progress you're making.

Now that you're tracking your wealth like a pro, let's talk about how to *enjoy* it along the way. In the next chapter, we'll explore the concept of mini-retirements — taking intentional breaks throughout your life to recharge, explore and live fully without waiting for traditional retirement. Because life isn't just about working and saving; it's about *living*. Let's find out how to make that happen now.

Chapter 11

Take MINI-RETIREMENTS

What if you could sprinkle moments of retirement throughout your life *right now* instead of waiting until you're 65? That's what mini-retirements are all about. Let me take you on a journey with a couple who lived it first-hand.

Two of my friends, a power couple in their 30s, Alex and Jamie, had their financial game *on point*. By 35, they hit financial independence. No more alarms, no more commutes. They had an amazing wedding, followed by an epic honeymoon: a two-month wanderlust-filled adventure through the cobblestone streets of Italy and the sun-drenched beaches of Greece.

Fast forward to their baby's first birthday. Over a piece of cake (and plenty of chaos from toddlers running around), I asked how their early retirement dream was going. Their answer shocked me: 'We went back to work part-time.'

'It turns out,' Jamie said, 'retirement isn't the vibe we thought it would be. After the first few months of Netflix marathons and family time, we got... bored. We were wondering what our purpose was. We needed something to challenge us and to give our days meaning.'

Alex and Jamie's experience taught me something life-changing: A lot of us are chasing retirement or early retirement, thinking that it will solve all our problems, but maybe there's more to it than that. In this chapter we go through the science behind work, and rest, and why mini-retirements could be the solution we're looking for.

That conversation solidified something I'd been thinking: life isn't just about reaching the destination. It's about enjoying the journey. And taking mini-retirements allows you to have the best of both worlds: moments of freedom now balanced with the purpose and structure work can bring. And that's what this chapter is all about.

What's coming up next...

In this chapter, we're flipping the script on traditional retirement. Why wait until you're 65 to live your dream life when you can sprinkle mini-retirements throughout your journey? Together, we'll explore:

- what mini-retirements are and why they're the ultimate life hack
- the science behind why too much work leads to burnout, but too much free time can leave you feeling lost
- how to afford mini-retirements without derailing your financial goals (hint: dual savings pools)
- clever strategies such as travel hacking and making your money work for you while you're off exploring the world
- real-life stories (including my own!) of using investments to fund epic adventures.

If you've ever dreamed of taking a career break, travelling the world or just pressing pause without the guilt, this chapter is your roadmap.

Science backs it: Burnout and boredom are real

The truth is, humans are wired for purpose, but we also need rest. Mini-retirements help strike that balance. Let's dive into the science behind why working too much sucks, but so does doing nothing at all.

Burnout: When the hustle becomes a health hazard

We've been sold this idea that hustling *nonstop* is the key to success, but research says otherwise. Burnout isn't just feeling tired, it's a full-blown mental and physical *breakdown* that can tank your health, happiness and even shorten your lifespan.

A massive meta-analysis published in the *International Journal of Environmental Research and Public Health* looked at 46 studies covering over 800 000 people across 13 countries. The researchers found that people who worked long hours had a 24.5 per cent higher risk of developing serious health issues, and a shocking 46.5 per cent increase in physiological health problems like heart disease and high blood pressure.

And it's not just about physical health. A report from the American Psychological Association found that burnout leads to chronic stress, depression and even cognitive decline. Basically, the more you overwork, the worse your brain and body function.

The takeaway? If your life is a never-ending to-do list, your body will eventually quit on you.

The paradox of too much free time: Boredom can break you

Now, on the flip side, imagine having all the time in the world. No work. No obligations. At first it's *bliss*. You finally get to binge-watch every show ever made. But after a few months, a strange feeling creeps in... *What am I doing with my life?*

Turns out, science backs this up, too.

A study published in *PLOS Medicine* explored the mental health effects of universal basic income (UBI): a policy where people receive free money from the government, no strings attached. You'd think unlimited free time would make people *happier*, right? Nope.

The study found that while financial stress decreased, mental health benefits dropped if people stopped working or engaging in purposeful activities. In other words, having enough money to quit your job *isn't enough*; we still crave meaning and structure in our lives.

Another analysis by Social Europe, which reviewed UBI trials worldwide, found that while people initially enjoyed the freedom, long-term happiness depended on having a sense of purpose, whether through work, volunteering or meaningful projects.

And if you're thinking, *Well, maybe retirement is different,* think again.

The Okinawa Centenarian Study, which has been running for decades, investigates why residents of Okinawa, Japan, live longer than almost anywhere else in the world. It found that one of their key secrets to longevity is *ikigai* — a strong sense of purpose (more on this on page 204). The study found that those who stayed engaged in meaningful work, hobbies or community activities well into old age lived longer, healthier and happier lives compared with those who fully retired with no structured activities.

A similar conclusion came from Harvard Health Publishing, which reviewed multiple studies and found that having a strong sense of purpose is directly linked to a longer lifespan. Their findings suggested that people who stay active (whether through work, volunteering or passion projects) are less likely to suffer from depression and cognitive decline, and even have lower mortality rates than those who retire without clear purpose.

What does this mean? We actually *like* having something to do! Too much free time with zero structure isn't freedom — it's *aimlessness*.

Whether it's a career, a creative pursuit or helping others, having purpose is non-negotiable for a fulfilling life.

The perfect solution? Mini-retirements

So, if hustling until you drop is terrible, and quitting work completely makes you miserable... what's the answer?

Instead of grinding for 40 years straight and then *hoping* to enjoy life later, why not take planned breaks throughout your career? Imagine:

- taking a three-month break to travel Europe
- spending six months learning a new skill
- taking a year off to work on a passion project.

The beauty of mini-retirements is they let you recharge *without* losing your sense of purpose. They prevent burnout *and* boredom, giving you the best of both worlds.

And the best part? You don't need to be a millionaire to do it. A simple savings plan and some flexibility can help you take that dream break way sooner than you think.

If you're stuck in the cycle of burnout or boredom, it's time to rethink the way you approach work. Mini-retirements aren't a luxury, they're a science-backed way to live a happier, more fulfilling life.

Dual savings pools

A lot of people think that once you invest or save money, it's locked away forever like some kind of financial black hole. But here's the thing: your money is yours, and you can access it whenever you need it.

That's why I love the dual savings pool approach: one for now and one for later. It gives you flexibility, freedom and financial security, all at the same time.

Let me share a story with you.

How we used our investments to travel the world

After Pablo and I bought our first home, we weren't exactly sure what our future plans were, but we knew we wanted to build wealth and give ourselves options.

Over time, we built up a solid investment portfolio, and then, one day, we decided to do something a little different — we used some of our investments to fund a three-month round-the-world trip.

Yep, we literally sold some of our investments and used that money to travel. And it was one of the best decisions we ever made.

We explored new places, experienced different cultures and made incredible memories — all without worrying about debt or dipping into emergency savings. And you know what? We *still* had plenty of investments left continuing to grow for our future.

Later on, we did the same thing when we needed a bigger home. We sold some investments to upgrade to a larger place that better suited our growing family. Again, this wasn't money that was 'locked away' — it was money we had built over time, and we could use it when it mattered.

The two types of savings (and why you need both)

We touched on this in Chapter 7, but the reason this saving approach worked so well is because we followed a *dual savings approach*. Essentially this means you separate your money with *intention* and each account has a specific purpose.

Pool #1: Saving for the short- to medium-term

Pool #1 is money you save in a way that you can easily access when you need it, such as investing in stocks or opening a high-interest savings account. The key is that you can access this money relatively quickly if you decide to travel, buy a home, take time off work or for sabbaticals or personal growth projects.

Pool #2: Long-term savings

Long-term savings are savings that you know you won't touch for a *looong* time. This money is for your financial future (you're welcome, future you). Your superannuation or retirement fund is a classic example of long-term funds you set up for the future.

Why this works so well

- Flexibility and freedom: You're not *just* saving for retirement, you're also setting yourself up for amazing life experiences along the way.
- Security for the future: Your long-term investments are still growing in the background, giving you peace of mind that you'll be set later in life.
- You're always prepared for life's big moments: Whether it's travelling, upgrading your home or funding a new adventure, you have the financial means to make it happen.

Give yourself options

Having investments doesn't mean you're locking your money away forever, it means you're giving yourself options. One day, you might want to travel the world, buy your dream home, start your own business or take time off for a sabbatical or parental leave.

And when you have both a now fund and a later fund, you can do all of these things—without stress, without regret, and *without sacrificing your financial future.*

That's why building wealth isn't just about retirement, it's about giving yourself the freedom to live life on your own terms.

How to afford your mini-retirement

A few years ago, when we decided to hit pause on our regular life and take a three-month round-the-world trip, it wasn't some first-class adventure (though, that would've been nice). We had to be smart with our money, so we got creative.

First, we packed up all our stuff and squeezed it into my dad's garage (cheers, Dad!). Instead of leaving our apartment empty, we rented it out. That way, we at least had some passive income coming in while we were off exploring.

When it came to accommodation, we mixed it up: sometimes we stayed in hotels, but other times we crashed on friends' couches (because nothing makes you appreciate a real bed like a few nights on a lumpy sofa). We also focused on cheaper countries where our money stretched further.

And because we weren't completely off the clock, we worked while we travelled. The beauty of running an online business is that we can do it from anywhere. Sure, we weren't as productive (let's be real, the beach was calling) and we made less than usual, but having a little income trickling in meant we weren't just draining our savings.

If the idea of breaking up your working years with some well-earned adventure sounds good to you, here are some tips to help you make it happen — without breaking the bank.

Using travel hacking

I still remember the exact moment I stumbled into the world of points hacking, and honestly, it felt like unlocking a secret cheat code for life.

I was working a corporate tech job, minding my own business, when a colleague casually dropped the bombshell that he had booked a business class flight for less than the price of an economy ticket.

'Wait... what?' I blinked at him in disbelief.

'It's really simple,' he said, as if revealing the most obvious thing in the world. 'You just get a points-earning credit card with a big sign-up bonus, put all your regular expenses on it, and as long as you pay it off before the interest-free period ends, you rack up points without paying a cent in interest. Boom—business class flights for free.'

I was sceptical. Surely the banks had figured this out? Surely there was some catch? But I went down the research rabbit hole, double-checking every little detail... and sure enough, it checked out.

It turns out, my financially savvy dad had already been on to something similar for years. I always saw him putting every expense on his credit card, then cashing in points every few months for free gift cards. But this method was next level.

I soon discovered that redeeming points for flights is the ultimate hack, because the value of your points skyrockets when used for travel. For example, let's say you have accumulated some points. If you redeem them for a gift card, they might be worth $500. If you redeem them for flights, they could be worth $2000+.

That's a x4 difference just by knowing where to spend them! And since flights are usually one of the biggest costs when travelling, this trick can slash your travel budget dramatically.

How we saved $10 000 on flights

When we took our round-the-world trip, we cashed in our points and it saved us over $10 000 on flights. That's money we could spend on experiences instead of airfares.

Want to try it yourself? Here's how:

How to hack your way to cheaper flights
- Find a rewards system: Look for frequent flyer programs that fit your travel style (like Qantas, Velocity or Amex).

- Get a points-earning credit card with a big sign-up bonus: Some cards give 100 000+ bonus points just for signing up and hitting the minimum spend.
- Put your everyday expenses on the card: Groceries, bills, subscriptions — everything goes on the card to rack up points faster.
- Always pay it off before interest hits: No free flights are worth paying huge interest rates — set up autopay so you never get charged.
- Redeem your points for flights (not gift cards!): This is where the real magic happens. Maximise your points by booking flights instead of opting for smaller rewards.

Start earning free travel now

Once you get the hang of points hacking, it's insanely addictive. We've used our points for business class flights, international getaways and even hotel stays — and trust me, once you fly business for free, it's hard to go back.

Things to be mindful of

Points hacking is amazing... when you do it right. If you don't play smart, the credit card companies *will* play you. Remember, banks aren't handing out free business class flights out of the goodness of their hearts. They make money when people don't pay off their full balance, rack up interest and get trapped in debt. Don't be that person.

Here's how to win the game without getting burned.

Always pay off your full balance before interest kicks in

This is the golden rule. Most rewards cards have crazy high interest rates (think: 20+ per cent), and if you carry a balance and have to pay interest back to the banks, you're hustling backwards, and any money you 'save' by using your points would quickly be eaten away by interest you need to pay back to the banks. Always set up autopay so your balance is cleared before the interest-free period ends.

Don't fall for the minimum payment trick

Ever noticed how your credit card statement says you only need to pay a tiny amount, like $50? That's how they trap people. Paying the minimum keeps you in debt forever, racking up insane interest along the way. Always pay the full balance — no exceptions.

Credit cards can make you spend more

Studies show that people tend to spend more when using a credit card compared to cash or debit. This is because it doesn't feel like you're spending your own money since it doesn't come out of your bank account immediately, so you don't feel the loss. On top of that, banks don't make it easy to track spending: apps and statements often lag (maybe on purpose...). So be extra mindful of how much you're actually spending.

Thinking of buying a house? Your credit limit could reduce your borrowing power

This is huge if you're planning to buy property. Many banks look at your full credit limit as debt, *even if you pay it back in full every month*. That means a having a credit card with a credit limit could reduce your mortgage borrowing capacity by up 6x the credit limit. So, for example, a $15 000 credit limit could reduce your borrowing capacity by $90 000 (double check with your lender). If you're applying for a home loan soon, consider lowering your credit limit or cancelling your card to avoid getting penalised.

How to travel more for less (without compromising on fun!)

Think travel is too expensive? Think again. The secret isn't just spending less — it's spending smarter. Here's how you can stretch your dollar *waaay* further while still living your best travel life.

Go to more economical countries

Imagine buying a bottle of water at a supermarket for $1. Now, take that same bottle and move it to an airport — suddenly it's $5. Put it at a festival, now it's $10. Same water, different price.

Travel works the same way. In some countries, your money stretches so much further, meaning you can enjoy amazing experiences at a fraction of the cost. A beachfront villa in Bali? Probably cheaper than a budget motel in Sydney.

A great resource to check out is numbeo.com, where you can compare the cost of living in different countries and find destinations that give you the most bang for your buck.

Travel off-peak and save big

Want to cut your costs by 30 per cent (or more) without sacrificing luxury? Travel during off-peak or shoulder seasons.

Not only are flights and accommodation *way* cheaper, but you'll also get:

- fewer crowds (no fighting for that perfect Instagram shot)
- lower prices on tours and activities (fewer people mean operators work harder to fill places)
- better service (since places aren't overwhelmed with tourists).

For example, Europe in September/October is still warm but way less packed than the chaotic summer months. Same vibes, less money. Win-win!

Stay with friends and family

If you have friends or family overseas, now is the time to cash in on those relationships (in the nicest way possible, of course).

Accommodation is one of the biggest travel expenses, so if you can crash with someone for even a few nights, you'll save hundreds (or thousands!) of dollars. Plus, staying with locals means:

- free insider tips on the best places to go
- home-cooked meals (goodbye overpriced tourist traps!)
- a cosy place to stay without breaking the bank.

And, hey, if you don't have anyone to stay with? Try house-sitting! Websites like trustedhousesitters.com connect travellers with people who need someone to look after their home or pets while they're away.

Work on the go (and get paid to travel)

Remote work isn't just a buzzword—for some people, it's the ultimate travel hack.

One of my friends works for a tech company, and he's mastered the art of 'work from anywhere'. Every year, he spends months travelling with his partner, combining:

- his company's remote work policy (so he still gets paid)
- annual leave for full travel days
- unpaid leave to extend his adventures.

The best part is he doesn't have to quit his job or drain his savings—he's funding his travels while still earning an income.

If you can work remotely, even part-time freelance gigs can help keep money coming in *while* you explore.

Your turn: Let's design your mini-retirement

So, what would you do if you didn't have to work? We're going to dive deep and make it real in this next exercise. You'll get a few journal prompts to help you take your first step towards your own mini-retirement.

Step 1: Imagine your mini-retirement

Imagine that you've just been given a three-month mini-retirement, fully funded. No work, no stress—just time to do what you want.

Write down your answers to these questions:

- Where would you go (if anywhere)?
- How would you spend your time?
- What's something you've always wanted to do?
- Who would you spend time with?
- How would you structure your time to make it meaningful?

Step 2: Find your ikigai

The Japanese concept of *ikigai* (a reason for being) is all about finding the sweet spot between what you love, what you're good at, what the world needs and what you can get paid for (see figure 11.1).

Figure 11.1: The ikigai balance

Draw four overlapping circles on a page and brainstorm:

- What do you love?
- What are you good at?
- What does the world need?
- What can you get paid for?

Look for something that appears in multiple circles. This could be your *ikigai* — your reason to wake up excited each day. Can you incorporate this into your mini-retirement?

Step 3: Take a mini-retirement day

If you're not ready for a full-on mini-retirement, could you try a mini-mini-retirement day instead? Here's how:

- Set aside one day to do something you'd do on your ideal mini-retirement.
- Block out your schedule and fully immerse yourself in it — no distractions.
- Reflect on how you felt and what you learned.

Step 4: Do it!

Here are some small steps you can take today to make your mini-retirement a reality.

- Start a mini-retirement savings fund.
- Research remote work or sabbatical options.
- Plan a budget-friendly version of your dream trip.
- Start a side hustle that allows flexibility.

Key takeaways

- Mini-retirements are like sprinkling little slices of retirement throughout your life: no need to wait until you're 65 to start living your dream.
- Burnout and boredom are two sides of the same coin: too much work drains you, but too much free time without purpose can leave you feeling lost.
- The key to balance is purpose + rest. Mini-retirements let you recharge without losing that sense of meaning.
- Dual savings pools (one for now, one for later) give you the freedom to fund adventures and secure your future.
- You can fund mini-retirements creatively through smart investing, part-time work, renting out property and even travel hacking with points.
- Celebrating life along the way is just as important as hitting big financial milestones. Your wealth is a tool to create memorable experiences, not just numbers on a spreadsheet.

In a nutshell

Mini-retirements let you enjoy life now instead of waiting until 65. The key is balance—too much work leads to burnout, but too much free time without purpose can leave you feeling lost. With smart planning, dual savings pools and travel hacking, you can take career breaks without derailing your financial goals. Wealth isn't just for someday—it's a tool to create freedom and fulfilment today.

Next, we'll explore the final piece of the puzzle: giving back. Because true wealth isn't just about what you gain, it's about the impact you leave behind.

Chapter 12
PAY IT FORWARD

No one is truly self-made. Every success story is stitched together with threads of kindness, generosity and support from others. Sometimes it's the small, unseen acts — the couch someone lets you crash on, the warm meal shared, the simple 'I'm here for you' — that create the biggest ripple effects.

Noah's story

Noah grew up in Melbourne with his single mum and sister. His mum had migrated to Australia, and while finances were tight, their small family made it work. Noah doesn't remember much about the very early years — there were some tough times — but as he got older, life settled into a more typical rhythm. What stood out most wasn't the struggle, but the strength of his mum's values.

His mum always reminded him how lucky they were to be in Australia. She never stopped appreciating the opportunities they'd been given — whether it was access to healthcare, education or a safe place to call home. And from a young age, she instilled in Noah the importance of giving back. She'd say, 'If you're ever in a position to help others, do it. We're here because others helped us.'

That message stayed with Noah as he got older.

After years of working in consulting, Noah found himself drawn to something more, something rooted in that gratitude he'd never shaken.

It started small. Noah and a friend would head out after work, buy fresh bread from a local bakery and hand it out to people sleeping rough on Melbourne's streets. Simple, right? Just bread. But what struck Noah wasn't the food, it was the conversations.

Some of the people they met hadn't spoken to anyone in days, weeks, even.

That realisation hit harder than any boardroom meeting or financial report ever could.

Noah decided to do more. He co-founded a charity called Mobilise, which isn't your typical charity. Mobilise isn't about soup kitchens or large-scale events (though those are incredibly valuable too). Noah's mission was direct, personal and immediate. Sometimes that meant providing someone with a warm meal or a care package; other times, it was bigger — like handing over cash to someone in crisis, no strings attached.

One story stuck with Noah more than any other. A woman with a baby, desperate to escape an abusive relationship, reached out to Mobilise. She had no money, no safety net and nowhere to go, but with the support from Mobilise, she didn't just leave — she rebuilt.

A small amount of financial aid covered her rent for a few months, giving her the breathing room to find a job, regain her independence and start a new chapter free from fear. It wasn't a grand gesture. It wasn't a headline-grabbing campaign.

It was just enough.

And sometimes, *just enough* is all it takes to change a life.

The ripple effect of kindness

Mobilise started small: just Noah, his friend and a few loaves of bread. But kindness has a funny way of growing.

A few years after its launch, Mobilise caught the attention of ultra-marathon runner Nedd Brockmann. Nedd isn't your typical weekend jogger — this guy was running from Perth to Sydney. Yep, you read that right: 4000 kilometres across an entire country.

And he decided to dedicate his run to raising funds for Mobilise.

Imagine that: The kindness that Noah experienced as a child inspired him to share bread with someone in need, and then it sparked a movement that inspired a man to run thousands of kilometres, raising money to help even more people. And with every dollar raised, Noah's charity was able to reach further, help more and continue the cycle of paying it forward.

Noah's story isn't just about hardship, charity or even success, it's about the interconnectedness of our lives.

There's a myth we love to tell ourselves of the 'self-made' person. The entrepreneur who pulled themselves up by their bootstraps. The billionaire who started with nothing. The overnight success that seems to have appeared out of thin air.

But here's the truth: No one does it alone.

Behind every success story are the people who opened doors, offered advice, shared resources or simply believed when no one else did. We're all, in some way, the product of the kindness of others — knowledge passed down. Support given freely. Opportunities shared.

And the most powerful thing we can do?

Pay it forward.

Because the ripple effect is real. It started with Noah's mum receiving kindness when she needed it most. It continued with Noah helping others through Mobilise. Then it grew through Nedd crossing a country to raise funds. And, now, it lives on in every life Mobilise touches.

Kindness doesn't stop. It keeps moving — through us, around us, beyond us.

The ripple effect in action

When you send that encouraging message, offer someone your time or lend a helping hand, you're doing more than just one good deed. You're setting off a ripple effect: a wave of kindness that can touch lives you'll never meet.

So the next time you're wondering if a small act of generosity matters, remember the science: *It does. More than you'll ever know.*

Your turn: Reflection prompt

- Think of a time when someone's kindness made a difference in your life. Did it inspire you to help someone else?
- How can you start a ripple of generosity today? Remember, it doesn't have to be big. A simple act can create waves.

What's coming up next...

In this chapter, we'll explore the transformative power of paying it forward — how small acts of kindness can create ripple effects that stretch far beyond what you'll ever see. You'll discover:

- why no one is truly self-made: every success story is woven with threads of generosity and support
- the ripple effect of kindness and how even the smallest acts can spark life-changing outcomes
- the science behind generosity: how helping others boosts your happiness, health and even success
- how to shift from a scarcity mindset to an abundance mindset, realising that sharing knowledge and wealth makes us all richer
- simple, powerful ways to pay it forward in your own life, starting today.

Because true wealth isn't just about what you have, it's about the impact you make. Let's dive in and start your ripple.

The science of paying it forward

Generosity isn't just a warm, fuzzy feeling; it's a superpower backed by science. Researchers have been obsessed with understanding how acts of kindness ripple through communities, influencing not just the people directly involved but even strangers several degrees removed. Think of it like tossing a pebble into a pond — the splash is small, but the ripples reach far and wide.

When you help someone, you're not just making their day, you're creating a chain reaction that can spread beyond what you'll ever see.

Here's what the science says about the incredible power of paying it forward.

Generosity is contagious (yes, like a good kind of virus)

One of the most fascinating studies on the ripple effect of kindness didn't happen in a lab or a boardroom. It happened in an unexpected place: a video game.

Picture this: a beautiful, ethereal world inside a massive multiplayer online role-playing game called *Sky: Children of the Light*. Think magical landscapes, floating islands and players from all over the world exploring together. But the real magic wasn't just in the graphics, it was in the generosity happening between players.

Researchers observed how players interacted in the game and what counted as an act of kindness. It was simple stuff, such as gifting in-game items (like candles or special powers), helping new players navigate tricky levels or understand the game mechanics or offering companionship: literally holding hands in the game to guide someone through dark, challenging areas.

What they found

Generosity is contagious, like, seriously contagious. Players who either received or even just witnessed acts of kindness were way more likely to pay it forward. It wasn't just a one-off thing, either: this ripple effect created a more connected, engaged and supportive community within the game.

And here's the best part: people didn't pay it forward because they felt obligated, they did it because it felt good. That warm, satisfying feeling you get when you help someone? It turns out it's universal, even in virtual worlds.

This mirrors real life perfectly. When you see someone perform an act of kindness, whether it's holding the door open, paying for a stranger's coffee or mentoring someone starting out, it subtly encourages you to do the same. It's like a social domino effect: one small push and the kindness keeps spreading.

Kindness doesn't stop with you. Even when you think no one's watching, your actions can inspire others in ways you'll never fully realise.

The pay-it-forward experiment: The chain reaction of kindness

Now, let's leave the video game world behind and step into a real-life experiment that proves kindness is more than just a feel-good moment — it's a chain reaction waiting to happen.

In this study, researchers wanted to see if the pay-it-forward phenomenon was more than just a cute idea. Could kindness really spark more kindness, even in a controlled environment where no one was expected to return the favour?

How the experiment worked

Participants were part of a simple game involving tokens that held real value:

- Player 1 received a valuable token and had a choice: keep it for themselves or pass it on to Player 2.
- Player 2, if they received the token, faced the same choice: keep it or pass it on to Player 3.

There was no catch. No rules saying they had to pass it on. No guilt trips. Just a simple choice: keep it or give it away.

The results

Many of the participants chose to pay it forward, but here's the fascinating part: even though there was no obligation to pass on the kindness, the emotional impact of being helped made people more likely to help someone else.

And get this — people didn't pay it forward because they were thinking, *Ooh, I bet this will create a ripple effect*. They did it because receiving kindness felt good, and they wanted to pass that feeling along. It was a natural, emotional response, not a strategic one.

What we learned from this

Kindness isn't transactional. It's emotional.

People pay it forward not because they have to, but because it feels good to do so. It's as though kindness leaves an imprint on your heart, and you can't help but want to share it.

Why does this happen? The psychology behind paying it forward

So, what's happening inside our brains when we experience or witness generosity? Spoiler alert: it's not just about being a 'good' person. There's actual neuroscience behind it.

The helper's high: Nature's feel-good drug

Acts of kindness trigger a release of feel-good chemicals in the brain, such as dopamine, oxytocin and endorphins. This cocktail of happiness creates what psychologists call the helper's high. It's that warm, fuzzy, almost euphoric feeling you get after doing something good for someone else.

Think of it like the emotional version of a runner's high, only you don't need to break a sweat to get it.

Social bonding: We're wired to connect

Humans are social creatures. Even the most introverted among us thrive on connection. When you help someone, you're not just performing a nice gesture, you're strengthening a social bond — even if it's with a stranger.

This sense of connection boosts your mood, reduces stress and creates a feeling of belonging, which is essential for mental wellbeing.

Identity and self-esteem: You become the person you admire

Here's a fascinating truth: generosity is a win-win. When you give, you feel good about yourself. You like the person you are. You respect your own choices, which fuels your self-esteem. This emotional reward is one of the best-kept secrets of living generously.

Generosity shapes how we see ourselves. When you're kind to others, you start to internalise the belief that you're a good, compassionate person. This reinforces your self-image, boosts your self-esteem and motivates you to keep acting in line with those values.

Whether it's leaving a generous tip, donating to a charity or mentoring someone who reminds you of your younger self, these acts of giving create a sense of fulfilment. Over time, they define your legacy — not just in material terms but in how you've made others feel.

It's like a positive feedback loop: You help someone → You feel good → You see yourself as a kind person → You want to do it again.

The long-term game: Why 'share' beats 'steal' in life

When it comes to life, business and relationships, there's one big question:

Is it better to be cutthroat and competitive, or kind and cooperative?

Should you focus on winning at all costs, or try to create win-win situations where everyone benefits?

Surprisingly, science has the answer, and it comes from one of the coolest experiments ever: The 'share or steal' simulation.

The experiment: A game that reveals how life works

Back in the 1980s, a political scientist named Robert Axelrod wanted to figure out which strategies work best when people have to decide whether to share or steal. So, he did something genius: he invited experts from around the world to create computer programs that would compete in a virtual tournament.

The rules were simple

Each program had to play a game where it could choose to either:

- share (work together)
- steal (take everything for itself)

The outcomes

- If both programs chose to share, they'd both get a pretty good reward.
- If one program chose to steal while the other shared, the stealer would get all the rewards, and the sharer would get nothing.
- If both chose to steal, they'd both get nothing.

The twist

This wasn't just a one-off game. The programs played multiple rounds against each other, meaning every choice affected future rounds. Would a program try to be sneaky and steal for quick wins? Or would it build trust by sharing, hoping the other would do the same?

The winning strategy: Tit for tat (aka, play nice… but not too nice)

So, which program came out on top?

It wasn't the sneaky ones that stole to get ahead.

It wasn't the ones that shared all the time, either.

The winner was a simple strategy called 'tit for tat'. Here's how it worked:

- Start by sharing: The program always started with a friendly move — choosing to share.
- Copy what the other player does: If the other program shared, it kept sharing. If the other program stole, it stole right back in the next round.
- Forgive quickly: If the other player went back to sharing, it forgave and shared again. No grudges.

Why it won

Ultimately, this strategy worked because it was:

- Friendly: It never started a fight.
- Fair: It didn't let anyone take advantage of it.
- Forgiving: If someone made a mistake but tried to make it right, it gave them another chance.

Even though other programs tried to cheat for quick wins, 'tit for tat' crushed them in the long run. Why? Because the sneaky programs eventually got shut out — no one wanted to play with them anymore. Meanwhile, the programs that shared built strong partnerships, leading to more rewards over time.

What this means for real life

This isn't just a lesson from some old computer game, it's a rule for life.

Quick wins vs long-term success

People who try to 'steal' their way to the top — whether in business, friendships or life — might get ahead for a little while. But over time, they lose something way more valuable: trust.

No one wants to deal with someone who's selfish, sneaky or only out for themselves.

Trust is everything

In business, relationships or even casual friendships, trust is like your secret superpower. When people know you're reliable and fair, they want to work with you, help you and stick around.

Win-win is the ultimate strategy

The people who truly 'win' in life aren't the ones who step on others to get ahead, they're the ones who lift others up as they rise.

- Entrepreneurs who build ethical businesses create loyal customers.
- Leaders who support their teams inspire people to go the extra mile.
- Friends who are kind and genuine create lifelong connections.

The big lesson: Life is a long game

Here's the truth: life isn't a one-time game. It's not about winning today and forgetting about tomorrow.

Every decision you make — every relationship, every deal, every conversation — is part of a bigger picture. And the people who play the long game by focusing on trust, kindness and fairness? They don't just survive. They thrive.

In the short term, stealing might seem like a shortcut. But in the long run, sharing wins every time.

Why it's important to pay it forward

Sometimes the most life-changing opportunities don't come from the perfect pitch or the boldest move. They come from a simple message, a genuine connection and the decision to pay it forward.

I still remember the nerves buzzing in my chest the day I sent the message.

I was just a student, interning at a small company, tasked with updating their blog. It was a simple assignment, but I wanted it to be more than just filler content. I wanted to create something meaningful, something that would stand out. So, I dove headfirst into the rabbit hole of LinkedIn, scrolling through endless profiles, searching for someone inspiring to interview.

That's when I found Ahmed.

Ahmed had gone to the same university as me, but that's where the similarities seemed to end. After graduation, he'd launched into a completely different stratosphere: founder and CEO of a wildly successful start-up, a company now valued in the hundreds of millions. To me, he felt untouchable, one of those names you read about in business magazines, not someone you'd ever expect to meet, let alone talk to.

Still, on a whim, I decided to shoot my shot.

I crafted a message — polite, professional, but probably a little awkward — and hit *send*. I didn't expect a reply. Why would someone like him respond to someone like me?

But then: *ping*. A reply.

Not only did Ahmed respond, but he was kind, thoughtful and surprisingly down-to-earth. He agreed to an interview.

What I thought would be a quick, formal chat turned into something much more. We scheduled a call, and instead of sticking to the usual business buzzwords, we had a genuine, heartfelt conversation. Ahmed shared his journey—growing up in Western Sydney, the child of immigrants, navigating the challenges of being part of a working-class family trying to find their place in a new country.

What struck me most was how *relatable* his story was. Ahmed didn't grow up dreaming of boardrooms or billion-dollar valuations. In fact, when he was at university, he didn't even know what the word *entrepreneur* meant. He stumbled into it almost by accident after attending an event hosted by the university's Entrepreneur Society. He was curious but clueless—kind of like me, fumbling through that internship, trying to figure out what I wanted to do with my life.

His start-up story wasn't glamorous. It wasn't the kind of thing Hollywood would make a movie about. It started as a simple textbook delivery service. No investors. No flashy office. Just Ahmed, his beat-up car and a whole lot of hustle, driving around the city, personally delivering books to students, one order at a time.

Fast forward a few years, and that scrappy little idea had grown into a multi-million-dollar business. But, despite all his success, Ahmed stayed grounded. No ego. No pretence. Just a genuine person who never forgot where he came from.

The lesson that changed everything

After our interview, we stayed in touch. Over time, Ahmed became more than just a contact, he became a mentor and a friend.

Years later, as I was building my own start-up (my budgeting tool Billroo) I found myself reaching out to Ahmed regularly—sometimes for advice on business strategy, sometimes just to vent about the rollercoaster that is entrepreneurship—and, every time, without fail, he'd respond. With wisdom. With encouragement. With the same generosity he showed me in that very first reply.

I once asked him, 'How can I ever repay you for all your help?'

He just smiled and said, 'Pay it forward.'

Those three words stuck with me.

What I didn't know at the time was that Ahmed's generosity wasn't a random act. Someone had done the same for him when he was starting out. Another entrepreneur had answered his cold message, shared their knowledge, and when Ahmed asked how he could repay the favour, they gave him the same advice: 'Pay it forward.'

And that's exactly what he's done — not just for me, but for countless others. Because that's the beautiful thing about kindness: it doesn't stop with you. It creates a ripple effect, touching lives in ways you'll never fully see.

Ahmed didn't reply to my message because he expected anything in return. He wasn't thinking about networking or leverage or future favours. He replied because someone once did the same for him. And now, I carry that lesson with me.

Whether it's mentoring someone just starting out, sharing what I've learned or even just replying to a message from a student who's nervous to hit send, I know that these small acts can change the trajectory of someone's life.

Because success isn't just about climbing the ladder. It's about reaching back down to pull others up with you.

The heart of paying it forward

As you move through this book (and through life) remember this: wealth isn't just measured in dollars, it's measured in the lives you touch, the knowledge you share and the impact you leave behind.

You don't have to wait until you've 'made it' to give back: your time, your insights, your encouragement are all powerful forms of currency. Sometimes, the simplest gesture (a reply to a message, a bit of advice, a kind word) can ripple through someone's life in ways you'll never fully understand.

So, here's my challenge to you: be someone's Ahmed.

Give back. Share your story. Pay it forward.

Because the ripple effect starts with you.

The abundance mindset: Why sharing makes everyone richer

I used to think I needed to keep my knowledge close like a secret recipe tucked away, afraid that if others found out, it would somehow lose its magic.

- What if sharing my secrets meant I couldn't use them anymore?
- What if there wasn't enough success or luck to go around?

That's what's called a *scarcity mindset*: the belief that there's only so much success, money or opportunity in the world. If someone else gets a slice, that must mean there's less left for the rest of us.

But here's what I've realised: the more you share, the more you help others, the more you get back in return.

Because money, success and wealth-building? They're not zero-sum games.

It's not like poker where, if you walk away with all the chips, it's because someone else lost theirs.

In fact, here's the mind-blowing truth about building wealth: We can all win at the same time.

The Apple shares example: Everyone can win

Let's say you buy shares in Apple. You're betting that the company will grow, right? Now imagine your friend also buys Apple shares.

If Apple grows, you both win.

If more people invest, Apple has more resources to be able to innovate, create new products and expand globally. This growth increases the company's value, which means your investment grows even more.

No one had to 'lose' for you to make money. Your gain didn't come from someone else's loss.

Everyone's slice of the pie got bigger because the pie itself grew.

The shift from scarcity to abundance

The scarcity mindset thinks:

- There's not enough to go around.
- If I share what I know, I'll lose my edge.
- Success is limited, so I have to hoard it.

But the abundance mindset knows:

- The more I give, the more I grow.
- Sharing knowledge doesn't diminish it, it multiplies it.
- Success isn't pie, it's like sunlight: there's more than enough for everyone.

When you adopt an abundance mindset, you realise that helping others succeed doesn't take anything away from you. In fact, it often brings even more opportunities your way — whether through collaboration, new ideas or simply the joy of seeing people thrive because of something you taught them.

Why it's important to share your knowledge (and this book!)

Imagine you've learned something life-changing, like the power of compound interest, investing or financial freedom. What's the point of keeping it to yourself?

- When you teach a friend about investing, you're giving them a gift that could change their life.
- When you show your family how to manage money, you're breaking cycles of financial stress for generations.
- When you share this book with someone, you're not just passing along information, you're starting a ripple effect that could impact countless lives.

Because here's the thing: knowledge doesn't run out when you share it.

It grows.

It spreads.

It compounds — just like wealth.

So don't just keep these lessons to yourself. Share what you've learned, talk about money with your friends and family, and if this book has helped you, pass it on.

Because at the end of the day, the real wealth isn't just in what you earn — it's in what you give back.

Your turn: Reflection

Take a moment to reflect on your life and your journey so far and write down your answers to the following prompts.

- Who has helped you along your journey? It could be a teacher, a mentor, a friend or even a stranger whose small act of kindness made a difference.
- How can you pay it forward today? It doesn't have to be big. Sometimes, the smallest gestures create the biggest ripples.
- Think of a time when someone's kindness made a difference in your life. Did it inspire you to help someone else?

Key takeaways

- No one is truly self-made: Every success story is built on a foundation of kindness, support and opportunities created by others.
- Kindness is contagious: A small act of generosity can create ripple effects that touch lives you'll never meet.
- The ripple effect is real: Whether it's a simple gesture or life-changing support, every act of kindness has the power to inspire more.
- Generosity isn't just good for others — it's good for you: Helping others boosts your happiness, strengthens connections and reinforces your sense of purpose.
- Wealth isn't just what you accumulate: It's also the impact you create, the lives you touch and the knowledge you share.
- Success is a positive-sum game: When you help others grow, you grow too. There's more than enough success to go around.

In a nutshell

As we've seen, wealth isn't just about dollars in the bank, it's about the ripples you create, the people you uplift, and the legacy you leave behind. The most powerful investment you can make is in others.

Now, as we head into the conclusion, we'll bring it all together. We'll reflect on the journey we've taken, the lessons learned, and how you can continue building a life of freedom, abundance and purpose.

LIVING THE FUN FINANCE FORMULA

As I write this, I'm in the back of a taxi in Vietnam, watching the world blur past — motorbikes weaving through traffic, rice paddies stretching endlessly and the hum of life in motion. It's the perfect moment to reflect on this journey we've taken together through these pages.

If there's one thing I want you to take away from this book, it's this: *you've got this*.

Money doesn't have to be stressful, dull or complicated. It can be fun, fulfilling and even a little addictive (in the best way possible), just like playing and winning at your favourite game. When you approach building wealth with a playful mindset, money becomes a tool that allows you to build a life where you're not just surviving but thriving — where your budget includes the things that make you happy, all while setting yourself up for the future at the same time.

Let's bring it all together

Throughout this book, I've taken you on a journey to discovering the Fun Finance Formula, and here's how it all comes together.

1. Discover that money is fun

People have mixed feelings about money — to some it's good, and to others it's bad. We learned that all these perspectives and feelings about money are correct because there are different types of money. But ideally, we want to focus on the fun and skilled money, because it's more in our control, easy to replicate and we enjoy earning and spending this type of money!

2. Master your money mindset

Your money mindset can either propel you forward or quietly hold you back. In Chapter 2 we discussed how the way you view money shapes your thinking and choices in life. You can change your viewpoint and avoid self-sabotage. Understanding how you relate to money can help you reframe your relationship with it.

3. Choose gratitude over comparison

True wealth isn't about flashy cars or designer bags — it's actually often what you don't see. Here we discussed how it's important to be grateful for what you have, and how you can use your own luck to your advantage. Acknowledging feelings, such as envy, can open you up to understanding what you want to achieve in life.

4. Set goals that excite you

It's so much easier to build wealth when you're excited about your goals and vision. We went through a visualisation exercise to help you identify what you truly want from life, and how to get there.

5. Spend with intention

A lot of people say 'money doesn't buy happiness' and in some ways it's true. You can't purchase meaningful relationships or a lifetime of happy memories, but there are some science-backed ways that you can spend that are more likely to make you happy. That's why it's important to spend with intention and align every dollar with your values.

6. Balance the 3Fs: Foundation, fun and freedom

It's important to balance all 3Fs in your budget, otherwise you'll feel stuck. For example, if you have foundation + freedom but no fun, you may feel burnt out and as though you're not enjoying yourself. If you have foundation + fun but no freedom, you may feel like you're not getting ahead. The key is to have balance.

7. Save without sucking the fun from life

Sometimes, saving money can be just as fun as spending it. When you treat it like a game and reward yourself along the way, you don't have to choose between enjoying life now and securing your future. You can have duel-savings pools — one for now and one for later — which allows you to enjoy life now and enjoy the future too.

8. Invest with confidence

If you make investing hard, you just won't do it. And by not investing, you'll actually be losing money (because of inflation and the rising cost of living). That's why it's important to create a simple investing strategy that works for you and, ideally, automate it.

9. Win the property game

If property is part of your wealth-building plan, having the right strategy can make all the difference. Whether you're buying your first home or growing an investment portfolio, property can be a powerful tool for financial freedom.

10. Track your wealth for fun

One of the best things you'll ever do for your motivation, and your finances, is tracking your net worth. If you don't track how far you've come, you'll *never* feel like you're making progress. And you'll always be chasing the next thing, forgetting that past you would be shook by how rich present you is.

11. Take mini-retirements

Why wait until you're in your 60s to enjoy life? Mini-retirements allow you to experience freedom throughout your life by taking breaks to reset, travel, explore and recharge while still building long-term wealth.

12. Pay it forward

True wealth isn't just about what you accumulate — it's about how you use it to uplift others. No one is truly self-made. Every success story is stitched together with threads of kindness, generosity and support from others. And the amazing thing about kindness and generosity is that it creates a ripple effect that benefits everyone.

Your turn: Next steps

Reading this book is just the beginning. Now it's time to put what you've learned into action. Here are three things you can do right now to start applying the Fun Finance Formula.

1. Pick one financial habit to implement this week: Whether it's tracking your spending, automating your savings or setting up an investing account, aim to just start.
2. Write down your financial 'why': What excites you about building wealth? What's the dream you're working toward? Keep it somewhere visible as a daily reminder.
3. Share what you've learned: Whether it's passing this book to a friend, discussing money with your partner or teaching a family member about investing, knowledge is most powerful when it's shared.

And while this is the last chapter, your journey doesn't stop here. In fact, it's *only just beginning*.

Here's to your fun, financial future. *You've got this.*
Queenie Tan

REFERENCES

Chapter 1

Capital Group n.d., 'Time, not timing, is what matters', Capital Group, https://www.capitalgroup.com/individual/planning/investing-fundamentals/time-not-timing-is-what-matters.html.

Lotto, The n.d., 'What are the chances of winning division one?', The Lotto, https://help.thelott.com/hc/en-us/articles/4422500461337-What-are-the-chances-of-winning-division-one.

O'Hara, D 2023, 'Brad Klontz is concerned with how experiences affect our relationship with money', https://www.apa.org/members/content/money-relationship.

Tregenza, H 2024, 'What happens if a person is struck by lightning as four people remain in hospital in Sydney', ABC News, https://www.abc.net.au/news/2024-02-20/heres-what-happens-when-you-are-struck-by-lightning/103487890.

Chapter 3

Agarwal, S, Mikhed, S, Scholnick, B 2018, 'Peers' income and financial distress: Evidence from lottery winners and neighboring bankruptcies', Federal Reserve Bank Philadelphia, https://www.philadelphiafed.org/search-results?pageStart=1&pageSize=12

&searchQuery=Peers%E2%80%99+Income+and+Financial+Distress%3A+Evidence+from+Lottery+Winners+and+Neighboring+Bankruptcies.

Brown J, Wong, J 2017, 'How gratitude changes you and your brain', Mind and Body, https://greatergood.berkeley.edu/article/item/how_gratitude_changes_you_and_your_brain.

Kubba, H, Ali, A 2020, 'Unfair advantage, How you already have what it takes to succeed', Profile Trade.

Rea, M 2019, 'Gratitude', Wellness News, https://health.ucdavis.edu/nursing/academics/studentwellness/pdfs/BIMSON_Newsletter-November_2019.pdf.

Write Words Win 2025, 'How your unfair advantage is your edge to jumpstart your success', Write Words Win, https://writewordswin.substack.com/p/how-your-unfair-advantage-is-your?utm_campaign=post&utm_medium=web.

Chapter 4

Chakravarthy, M 2017, 'Modifying risks to improve outcome in cardiac surgery: An anesthesiologist's perspective', *Annals of Cardiac Anaesthesia*, vol. 20, no. 2, pp 226-33.

Csikszentmihalyi, M 2008, *Flow: The psychology of optimal experience*, Harper Perennial.

Matthews, G 2007, 'The impact of commitment, accountability, and written goals on goal achievement', Dominican University of California.

Patel, MS, Small, DS, Harrison, JD, Fortunato, MP, Oon, AL, Rareshide, CA, Reh, G, Szwartz, G, Guszcza, J, Steier, D, Kalra, P, Hilbert, V 2019, 'Effectiveness of behaviorally designed gamification interventions with social incentives for increasing physical activity among overweight and obese adults across the united states: the STEP UP randomized clinical trial', *JAMA Internal Medicine*, vol. 9, pp. 1-9.

Chapter 5

Aknin, LB, Dunn, EW, Proulx, J, Lok, I, Norton, MI 2020, 'Does spending money on others promote happiness? A registered replication report', *Journal of Personality and Social Psychology: Attitudes and Social Cognition*, vol. 119, iss. 2, pp, e15-e26.

Australian Fashion Council 2022, Seamless clothing stewardship scheme, AFC, https://ausfashioncouncil.com/program/seamless/.

Cornell Chronicle 2014, 'Doing makes you happier than owning – even before buying', https://news.cornell.edu/stories/2014/09/doing-makes-you-happier-owning-even-buying.

Firozi, P 2014, '378 people "pay it forward" at Starbucks', *USA Today*, https://www.usatoday.com/story/news/nation-now/2014/08/21/378-people-pay-it-forward-at-fla-starbucks/14380109/.

United States Environmental Protection Agency 2024, Textiles: Material specific data, EPA, https://www.epa.gov/facts-and-figures-about-materials-waste-and-recycling/textiles-material-specific-data.

Waldinger, R, Schulz, M 2023, 'What the longest study on human happiness found is the key to a good life', *The Atlantic*, https://www.theatlantic.com/ideas/archive/2023/01/harvard-happiness-study-relationships/672753/.

Chapter 7

Biospace 2018, 'New research suggests frequent rewards can be an effective motivation strategy, and can improve performance at work', BioSpace, https://www.biospace.com/new-research-suggests-frequent-rewards-can-improve-motivation-performance-at-work.

Wang, W, Li, J, Sun, G, Cheng, Z, Zhang, X 2017, 'Achievement of goals and life satisfaction: The mediating role of perception of successful agency and the moderating role of emotion reappraisal', *Psychology: Research and Review*, iss. 30, no 25.

Chapter 8

Coleman, M 2024, 'Dalbar QAIB 2024: Investors are still their own worst enemies', Index Fund Advisors, https://www.ifa.com/articles/understanding-investor-behavior-portfolio-performance.

S&P Global, Spiva, S&P Global, https://www.spglobal.com/spdji/en/research-insights/spiva/about-spiva/?utm_medium=undefined&utm_source=chatgpt.com&utm_campaign=undefined&utm_term=undefined&utm_content=undefined&gclid=undefined.

Morningstar 2024, US active/passive barometer report: mid-year 2024, Morningstar, https://www.morningstar.com/lp/active-passive-barometer.

Vanguard 2024, 2024 Vanguard index chart, Vanguard, https://fund-docs.vanguard.com/AU-Vanguard_Index_Chart_poster.pdf.

Chapter 9

APRA n.d., Financial claims scheme, APRA, http://apra.gov.au/financial-claims-scheme-0.

Chapter 10

Invest With Queenie n.d., Net worth tracker, Invest With Queenie, https://www.investwithqueenie.com/net-worth-tracker.

Chapter 11

American Psychological Association 2023, 'Employers need to focus on workplace burnout: Here's why', APA, https://www.apa.org/topics/healthy-workplaces/workplace-burnout.

Bilodeau, K 2019, 'Will a purpose-driven life help you live longer?', Harvard Health Publishing, https://www.health.harvard.edu/blog/will-a-purpose-driven-life-help-you-live-longer-2019112818378.

De Schutter, O, Van Parijs, P 2024, 'Can universal basic income really improve mental health?', Social Europe, https://www.socialeurope.eu/can-universal-basic-income-really-improve-mental-health-the-surprising-results-are-in.

Okinawa Research Center for Longevity Science n.d., Homepage, ORCLS, https://orcls.org/.

Thomson, RM, Kopasker, D, Bronka, P, Pchiardi, M, Khodygo, V, Baxter, AJ, Igelstrom, E, Pearce, A, Leyland, AH, Katikireddi, SV 2024, 'Short-term impacts of universal basic universal income on population mental health inequalities in the UK: A microsimulation modelling study', *PLOS Medicine*, vol. 21, iss. 3, e1004358.

Wong, K, Chan, AHS, Ngan, SC 2019, 'The effect of long working hours and overtime on occupational health: a meta-analysis of evidence from 1998 to 2018', *International Journal of Environmental Research and Public Health*, vol. 16, iss. 12.

Chapter 12

Hardial, N 2022, Sky: Children of the Light: 'A game about compassion and generosity', Kingsley Voice, https://kingsleyvoice.com/6143/entertainment/video-games-tech/sky-children-of-the-light-a-game-about-compassion-and-generosity/.

Levitt, SD, Levey, M 2021, 'Robert Axelrod on why being nice, forgiving, and provokable are the best strategies for life', Freakonomics, https://freakonomics.com/podcast/robert-axelrod-on-why-being-nice-forgiving-and-provokable-are-the-best-strategies-for-life/.